The Legal Rights
of Students

NASW PRESS

National Association of Social Workers
Washington, DC

James J. Kelly, *PhD, ACSW, LCSW, President*
Elizabeth J. Clark, *PhD, ACSW, MPH, Executive Director*

The Legal Rights of Students

General Counsel Law Note

Carolyn I. Polowy, JD
NASW General Counsel

Sherri Morgan, JD, MSW
NASW Associate Counsel

M. Scott Fisher, Jr.
Law Clerk

Alison Keller-Micheli
Law Clerk

Meghan Moore
Law Clerk

Andrew Rogers
Law Clerk

N A S W · LDF
National Association of Social Workers
Legal Defense Fund

NASW Press

Cheryl Y. Bradley
Publisher

Lisa M. O'Hearn
Managing Editor

This project was funded in part by the Aileen Neely bequest to the
NASW Legal Defense Fund.

Table of Contents

Introduction

It is the position of the National Association of Social Workers (NASW) that the nation's school systems are responsible for providing "all students with free, appropriate, quality education" to prepare them for full, productive, and intelligent participation in society on reaching adulthood.[1] The U.S. Constitution does not explicitly guarantee the right to an education;[2] however, denying children an education would deny them "the ability to live within the structure of our civil institutions, and [would] foreclose any realistic possibility that they will contribute … to the progress of our nation."[3]

School social workers are significant contributors to the formative years of children in U.S. schools. In many school systems across the country, school social workers are among a select group of professionals who are able to address the "personal and social problems that inhibit a student's ability to learn."[4] Furthermore, the role of the school social worker has evolved into a link between the family, the school, and the community.[5]

This law note reviews a number of the legal issues that affect the practice of social workers within the schools and under the multitude of jurisdictions that exercise control over public and private schools. Generalizations do not provide answers to specific legal problems in a particular school.

Reference often must be made to the layers of local, state, and federal laws and regulations which frequently change, and to the requirements of credentialing bodies. This law note is not intended to be a substitute for consultation with an attorney regarding specific issues that affect social workers.

History Of School Social Work

The history of school social workers dates back to the early 20th century, when the social work profession was still very new to U.S. society. Initially, school social work services were not provided by the school, but through private agencies and organizations.[6] It was not until 1913 that school systems began to establish school social work services.[7]

Early school social workers tended to focus on student attendance and enforcement of child labor laws.[8] As the educational system's structure—and the issues pertaining to children in the United States—began to develop and became more complex, so did the roles of school social workers. Toward the middle of the century, the profession's prestige transformed, and school social workers' roles shifted from "truant officers" to "caseworkers."[9]

By the 1980s, the scope of the services school social workers provided began to expand, as the educational, social, and economic needs of the nation's youth changed.[10] The number of "at-risk children in public schools" increased dramatically, augmenting the range of services that they required.[11] Today, school social workers' expertise in addressing students' psychosocial issues supports the school system in its primary function of effectively educating all students.[12]

School Social Worker Credentials

A s the need for school social workers' expertise increased, so did the number of surrounding legal issues. Legislatures and licensing boards responded to the expanding role for school social workers by developing new ways of regulating the practice.

Some states have created a separate school social worker credential; some accept the NASW school social worker credential. Still others require a teaching or student services credential. Some states lay out the qualifications for school social workers in statutes, rather than requiring a particular credential. Because states can vary so widely in their regulation of school social workers, practitioners need to be aware of their states' rules. For a detailed listing of school social worker statutes, see Appendix A.

A designated credential in school social work establishes a legal standard for delivering services in an educational environment. Attainment of a license or certification usually means that the social worker completed a sufficient amount of specialized training and education to work within a school system, as discussed below.[13]

NASW School Social Work Standards and Credentialing

In 1978, *NASW Standards for School Social Work Services* (hereafter, *Standards*) was drafted to provide practice standards and to further recognize the role of the school social worker.[14] Because of the nature of the school social work specialty's evolving practices and policies, NASW revised the *Standards* in 1992 and 2002.[15]

The Association sought to reinforce current practices for school systems that followed the *Standards*, and to provide a challenge to school systems that did not have similar principles in place.[16] The *Standards* also validated the "uniqueness and diversity of school social work as a specialty practice area," and confirmed the value of school social workers in assisting students "to achieve maximum benefits from their educational experiences."[17]

In addition to the *Standards*, in January 2000, NASW began to offer a school social work certification.[18] To qualify as an NASW Certified School Social Work Specialist, an applicant must:

- Earn a Master of Social Work (MSW) degree from a university accredited by the Council on Social Work Education (CSWE),[19]

- Complete at least two academic years (2,160 hours) of postgraduate, supervised school social work experience in a school setting,[20] and

- Be currently licensed as a social worker or a school social worker.

State Licensing or Credentialing Standards

NASW's credentialing requirements are on a voluntary basis, and are not binding in most jurisdictions. Since the inception of the school social work credentialing program, at least two states, Kentucky and Washington, have promulgated rules that require school social workers to be certified by NASW.[21]

Many states now have statutes requiring school social workers to meet that state's specific criteria for specialized licenses or credentials. As Appendix A shows, 38 states and the District of Columbia have set standards for social workers to practice in schools in their jurisdictions. In addition to separate certification, these standards include other specific requirements, which are discussed below, and are referenced in Appendix A.

Among the states that issue licenses and credentials to practice as a school social worker, 24 jurisdictions require the applicant to hold an MSW degree.[22] Idaho is an exception, because it requires applicants to hold either an MSW or a "master's degree in guidance and counseling, sociology, or psychology plus thirty semester hours of graduate work in social work education."[23]

An additional 13 states issue school social work licenses or credentials to social workers who have received a Bachelor of Social Work (BSW) degree.[24] In states such as Georgia, Maine, and New York, however, applicants who have a BSW must be pursuing an MSW to obtain a provisional school social worker license or credential.[25] The provisional licenses are usually valid for a period of three to five years. The school social worker must complete an approved MSW program prior to receiving a permanent or professional license.

In addition to the educational requirements listed above, other common criteria exist for school social worker certification found among the states, including:[26]

- Coursework in areas specific to social work (e.g., cross-cultural communication,[27] special education,[28] social welfare policy,[29] and human behavior in social environments[30]);

- A practicum or internship in a school setting (the number of required hours varies by state); and

- A passing score on an examination related to the social work profession.

Exemptions from State Board of Social Work Licensing Requirements

In many states, certain groups that practice social work are exempt from having to meet the requirements of state social work licensing boards.[31] This exemption extends to school social workers in at least 14 states.[32] Some states substitute social work board licensing requirements with board of education certification.

For practitioners who are exempted, restrictions are usually put in place to prevent them from practicing outside of their school systems without being licensed by the state board of social work examiners.[33] For a detailed listing of these exemptions, see Appendix A.

Legal Rights within the Public Education System

Right to Public Education

In *Brown v. Board of Education*,[34] the U.S. Supreme Court noted that education—as the principal means of teaching the child cultural values and vocational or career skills—is "perhaps the most important function of state and local government."[35] In *Brown*, the Supreme Court held that segregation of children in public schools solely on the basis of race deprives the children of the minority group of equal educational opportunities. Such segregation is, therefore, a violation of the "equal protection clause" of the Fourteenth Amendment.[36]

The Supreme Court recognized the importance of public education by emphasizing its role in U.S. society: "It is a principal instrument in awakening the child to cultural values, in preparing him for later professional training, and in helping him adjust normally to his environment … it is doubtful that any child may reasonably be expected to succeed in life if he is denied the opportunity of an education."[37]

Furthermore, in *Plyler v. Doe*, the Supreme Court held that it was prohibited for a state to deny public education to children who were not "legally admitted" into the United States.[38] The court noted that public education is not "merely some governmental 'benefit' indistinguishable from other forms of social welfare legislation. Both the importance of education in maintaining our basic institutions, and the lasting impact of its deprivation on the life of the child, mark the distinction."[39]

Last, it is possible for public school systems to develop school districts with an eye toward achieving a diverse student population. The Supreme Court recently decided a case involving the issue of whether public school districts, on a voluntary basis, can use race to justify the selection and admission of students to public schools in the name of achieving diversity.[40] The school districts involved in this case were using classifications of "white and nonwhite" and "black or other" to determine what schools students should be assigned to, within the given schools districts.[41]

Although the plurality opinion of the Supreme Court found that state governments do not have a compelling interest in achieving diversity within public schools,[42] Justice Kennedy's opinion concurring in the judgment is perhaps more influential.[43] Agreeing with the plurality, Kennedy found that: (1) the school districts' diversity initiatives were too broad and imprecise, and (2) their use of race-based classifications to achieve diversity was arbitrary and inconsistent.[44]

However, Kennedy maintained that schools do indeed have a compelling interest in achieving diversity, and may continue to pursue the goal of achieving student bodies of diverse backgrounds through race-neutral means. Kennedy suggested that this could be done by:

- Creating school districts based on community demographics,
- Developing new schools in certain neighborhoods,
- Recruiting specific students and faculty, and
- Using statistics to track enrollments and performance by race.[45]

With this guidance, the door is still open for school districts to pursue the goal of diversifying their student bodies.

Parental Rights

Providing public education is a paramount function of a state, but this responsibility must yield to parents' legal rights to make decisions concerning their children's education. For example, in *Pierce v. Society of the Sisters*,[46] the Supreme Court determined that a state statute compelling children between 8 and 16 years old to attend a public school unreasonably interfered with their parents' rights to make child-rearing decisions.

Citing the First Amendment right to freedom of religious expression,[47] the Supreme Court held that not allowing parents to "direct the upbringing and education of children under their control" was unconstitutional.[48] Parents have the liberty to choose to send their children to religious or public schools, and the state cannot infringe on that right. Although *Pierce* was decided more than 80 years ago, the court never overruled the decision or revoked this parental right.

Parental Rights and Religious Education

In U.S. society, parental decisions concerning the religious upbringing and education of their children are highly regarded.[49] Therefore, a state's interest in the education of children must be balanced with these parental interests, with respect to children's religious development.[50] The Supreme Court has held that laws requiring school attendance beyond the eighth grade may encroach on the First Amendment's "free exercise of religion clause."[51]

In *Wisconsin v. Yoder*, Amish parents demonstrated:

1. That compulsory school attendance past the eighth grade would place their children in an environment hostile to their religious beliefs, causing "a serious barrier to the integration of the Amish child into the Amish religious community," and

2. That "accommodating their religious objections by foregoing one or two years of compulsory education would not impair the physical or mental health of the child, nor result in an inability to be self-supporting."[52]

The application of this decision has been limited, however, to communities similar to the Amish.[53]

A recurring topic concerning public school education is a state's ability to introduce religion into its educational curriculum. The Supreme Court has consistently held that religion in the educational curriculum violates the Constitution's "establishment clause."[54]

In *Engel v. Vitale*, the Supreme Court prohibited a state from authorizing prayer in public schools.[55] The court also invalidated state laws requiring an equal time for creation science when teaching evolution in the science classroom,[56] and banned benedictions and prayers in public school graduation ceremonies.[57]

Despite the Supreme Court's reluctance to allow for religion in the public school setting, the court upheld it under certain circumstances. Recently, the court permitted state-funded educational voucher programs allowing parents to send their children to private schools, including parochial institutions.[58] The court noted that the program, which is neutral with respect to religion and provides assistance to a broad class of citizens, "permits ... individuals to exercise genuine choice among options public and private, secular and religious."[59]

Homeschooling and Mandatory School Attendance

If a student does not attend an established school system, homeschooling "often closes the door on providing key social work interventions and precludes third-party advocates for children."[60]

Because of this lack of oversight, some critics of homeschooling argue that parents may choose to homeschool their children to avoid the detection of child abuse.[61] Social workers should respect parents' rights to-choose the best educational settings for their children, and should support parents' choices for homeschooling. They should also, however, remain aware that opportunities for oversight may be limited.[62]

Compulsory school attendance laws exist in every state.[63] Theoretically, a parent's failure to send a child to school could subject the parent to review under the state's abuse and neglect laws.[64] In recent years, legislative and judicial recognition of parents' rights to homeschool their children has increased. Currently, all 50 states and the District of Columbia allow some form of homeschooling.

Because this area of law is relatively new, state case law regarding homeschooling is sparse and inconsistent. Few state cases exist, and the Supreme Court has not ruled on any aspect of the issue.[65]

The majority of states explicitly exempt homeschooling from compulsory school attendance laws.[66] However, the exemption from compulsory school attendance is generally granted only if the home-education plan meets specific statutory requirements.[67]

The 13 states that have not passed legislation explicitly providing for home-schooling generally allow homeschooling that is "substantially equivalent" to the education a child would receive in the public school.[68] A small group of states have determined that homeschools may qualify as private schools.[69]

In states that treat homeschools as private schools, the homeschool must meet all of the requirements of a private school. Thus, these states are the most demanding in their treatment of homeschools. For example, Nebraska's statute requires that all homeschools be approved and accredited.[70] Likewise, Alabama requires that homeschools, as private schools, have a state certification. Alabama also requires parent-teachers to be certified teachers.[71]

According to a U.S. Department of Education report, approximately 1.1 million students were being homeschooled in the United States in 2003.[72] Now that the basic right of a parent to homeschool his or her child is established in every state, many parents are now also asserting their children's rights to participate in extracurricular activities in public school settings.[73]

Generally, homeschooled students have been unsuccessful at securing the right to participate in extracurricular activities on constitutional grounds.[74] However, some states have enacted statutes that allow homeschooled students to participate in extracurricular activities in the public schools.[75] Given this ambiguity, the question of whether school-based social work services or counseling could be obtained by homeschooled children remains an open issue.

Right to Special Education Services

NASW supports "the right of every individual with a disability to obtain an education and advocates for public and private educational entities to ensure the least restrictive environment for people with disabilities in their educational endeavors."[76] Furthermore, NASW supports programs that improve the competence of social workers to work with people with disabilities, and "promotes the opportunity to educate people with disabilities to work in all areas of social work."[77]

Individuals with Disabilities Education Act

The Individuals with Disabilities Education Act (IDEA), formerly named the Education for All Handicapped Children Act, requires that a child with a disability be provided a "free appropriate public education."[78] Under IDEA, a free, appropriate public education is defined as "special education and related services."[79]

"Related services" include the transportation, speech pathology, physical and occupational therapy, social work, and medical services necessary to help each child benefit from instruction.[80] The provision of these services is decided on through a collaborative process, which results in each child's "individualized education program."[81]

Special education and related services must be provided to 3–21-year-old children with disabilities at no cost to parents, and under supervision of a government entity.[82] However, it is important to note that a school district is not required to provide the best possible education for a child under IDEA—only a "free and appropriate" one.[83] Therefore, many state and federal courts have addressed the question of what constitutes services that must be provided under IDEA.[84] Generally, courts have determined the services required on the basis of facts and circumstances of individual cases.

IDEA also provides that school districts must offer students with disabilities a free, appropriate, public education "in the least restrictive environment."[85] The "least restrictive environment" requirement has been interpreted to mean that a school district must teach a child with a disability in the same classroom as nondisabled children, to the maximum extent possible.[86] However, if the nature of the child's disability makes it impossible to educate the child in an integrated environment, the "least restrictive environment" requirement may be met if the child is placed in a segregated special education classroom or private school.[87]

In addition to the right to a "free appropriate education" in the "least restrictive environment" under IDEA, children with disabilities are also protected from discrimination in educational opportunities by two federal statutes—the Rehabilitation Act and the Americans with Disabilities Act.[88] The Rehabilitation Act applies to any school, public or private, receiving federal funds, whereas the Americans with Disabilities Act applies to any public school, whether or not it receives federal funds.

The regulations for each of these federal statutes require that a covered educational institution must provide a student with a disability with "reasonable accommodations."[89] The institution may also make "reasonable modifications to policies, practices, or procedures"[90] necessary to avoid discrimination based on the disability. Accommodations or modifications may include the following:

- Extra time to take examinations,
- The ability to retake an examination,
- A modified curriculum or alternate courses,
- A waiver of minimum grade point average,
- Permission to attend classes part time, or

■ Use of auxiliary aids.[91]

Furthermore, an accommodation or modification is considered reasonable as long as it "would enable the student to meet the educational institution's essential eligibility requirements," and would not require the public or private school to fundamentally change its program or standards.[92] However, like the services required under IDEA, courts generally determine what accommodations or modifications are reasonable on a case-by-case basis.

Under IDEA, if a child in need of special education and related services is enrolled in a private school, there are special situations in which states may be responsible for that child's tuition costs. First, if the state approves a parent's request to have a child placed in a private school, then the state will absorb the expenses.

Second, the state must assume the cost of sending the child to a private school if it is determined by state and local educational authorities that a private school placement is the only way a free appropriate public education may be provided.

IDEA, however, is silent on whether reimbursement for private school tuition is appropriate when parents place a child in a private school without state approval.[93] In *Burlington School Committee v. Department of Education*,[94] the Supreme Court determined that parents who unilaterally place a child in private school without state approval might still be entitled to reimbursement of the private school tuition costs under IDEA. However, the court conditioned tuition reimbursement on a determination by the courts that the IEP proposed by the school district was not appropriate.[95]

In another case, *Florence County School District Four v. Carter*,[96] the Supreme Court determined that parents who place their child in an unapproved (i.e., unaccredited) private school are still entitled to tuition reimbursement if (1) the proposed IEP was inappropriate, (2) the private school education was appropriate, and (3) the cost of the placement was reasonable.[97] The question remains before the courts, however, whether students must try and fail in proposed IEP placements before parents can unilaterally place them in private schools and claim tuition reimbursement.[98]

With these statutory requirements in mind, it is important to note the crucial role school social workers can play in the implementation of IDEA on a daily basis. Social work services may be used in any or all stages of the process mandated under IDEA.

School social workers are often involved at the initiation of the IEP process by identifying and assessing academically challenged students.[99] Furthermore, as students are identified and enter into the IEP process, school social workers may serve as members of the multidisciplinary team, participating in the decision-making process for the child's educational placement.[100]

Additionally, social workers are uniquely qualified by their cultural competence training to deal with diversity and cultural issues in special education. In spite of IDEA's specific prohibition on such, there are inequities for minority students in the provision of special education services.[101] Furthering this disparity is the disproportionate rate at which minority children are placed in restrictive, rather than integrated, special education settings.[102] This bias in the integration of children in special education violates not only IDEA, but also the social work ethic of cultural sensitivity.

School social workers have an obvious role to fill regarding these imbalances. Their cultural competence allows them to better identify and assess student needs. This focus on nonacademic factors allows social workers to look more broadly at a student's qualifications and placement in special education, focusing on the least restrictive placement possible.[103]

Thus, here and in broader contexts, school social workers can use their training and assessment skills to advocate for the least restrictive educational placements. To the extent appropriate, they may also promote the inclusion of students with disabilities in regular classrooms and activities.[104] In addition to advocacy on behalf of students, school social workers may help parents better understand, and advocate for, their children's rights.[105]

Finally, a school social worker's services and assessment may become a part of a student's IEP. For example, an emotionally disturbed student may be entitled to counseling services under an IEP, which can be provided in the school setting by the school social worker.[106] A school social worker may also be responsible for program monitoring and continued IEP evaluation.[107] Given the critical role that school social workers play in the implementation of IDEA, it is key that they understand the statute's requirements and goals.

Instruction in English versus Instruction in Student's Native Language

According to the Department of Education, in 2003–2004, approximately 4,999,481 English language learners (ELLs) were enrolled in pre-K–12th grade.[108] An English language learner is a student "whose first language is not English and who [is] in the process of learning English."[109]

This statistic mirrors the estimated 10 million residents nationally who are not fluent in English.[110] These students may be denied meaningful participation in the education process as a result of their language barrier. The Supreme Court has held that this is an unacceptable infringement of these students' civil rights.

In *Lau v. Nichols*, the Supreme Court held that denying students not fluent in English an education similar to native English-speaking students constitutes discrimination based on race, color, or national origin, thus violating the Civil Rights Act of 1964.[111] The court went on to say that, in such cases, school districts are required to take "affirmative steps to rectify the language deficiency."[112]

With this decision the Supreme Court imposed on school districts an obligation to provide English as a second language (ESL) services and programs for English language learners. The court did not, however, proscribe what specific services or programs should be implemented.

The English-language-only movement has been historically directed at Latino and Asian citizens and noncitizens. School social workers' advocacy may benefit English language learners in this matter.[113] One form of accommodating English language learners is to allow for instruction in the native language while the student transitions to English.

These programs are commonly referred to as bilingual education, and have been found to provide many advantages for students.[114] For example, studies conducted in the 1980s and 1990s demonstrated that non-English speaking children whose language is academically supported are able to achieve higher language development in the second language, compared to children who are instructed only in the second language.[115]

In addition, maintaining a native language could be advantageous because it helps a child to "value his/her culture and heritage, which contributes to a positive self-concept."[116] The child will also maintain the ability to communicate with the native-language community.[117] The end result is that the student will work at his or her actual level of intellectual ability, regardless of the level of proficiency in English.[118]

Rights of Immigrant Children

Immigration and the educational rights of immigrant children are closely related to language issues in the schools. In *Plyler v. Doe*, the Supreme Court struck down a Texas statute that prohibited undocumented immigrant children from attending public schools.

In extending public education to noncitizens and prohibiting discrimination based on legal status in this context, the Supreme Court recognized the costs of denying public education to immigrant children, and the fundamental unfairness in punishing them for a decision that was not theirs.[119] The court speaks strongly about the lifelong burden and disability of a lack of education—not only for the child, but also for society as a whole.[120]

Although the Supreme Court preserved access to public education for undocumented immigrant children, they still face significant challenges once enrolled. In 2001, U.S. Congress passed the No Child Left Behind Act (NCLB).[121] The regulations enacted to implement NCLB require the annual testing of schoolchildren, as well as condition-increased school funding based on high test scores.[122] This score-focused approach may lead to an even further decrease in resources for immigrant children and ELLs, and could result in greater prejudice against having such students in one's school.[123]

All school personnel are confronted with the issues surrounding and affecting immigrant children, especially school social workers who are in a unique position to recognize and advocate for immigrants. Although they are interested in developing public policy for continued access to public education for all children, regardless of legal status,[124] school social workers pay special consideration to the needs of immigrant children on a direct service level.

They can provide case management and referrals to services like translators, food programs, and health services.[125] School social workers can also provide culturally sensitive mental health services, and are encouraged to serve as a source of information to the administration, conveying immigrant students' unique needs and concerns.[126]

Rights of LGBT Students

Recognition and Support for LGBT Students

NASW has long recognized that prejudices aimed at lesbian, gay, bisexual, and transgender (LGBT) people can be harmful in many ways, and is "committed to advancing policies and practices that will improve the status and well-being of all lesbian, gay, and bisexual people"[127] as well as "those sometimes called 'transgender'".[128] In the school system, students need to be provided educational opportunities that afford them opportunities to understand and accept differences in, among other things, sexual and gender orientation.[129]

NASW takes the position that school environments that are nurturing and supportive of all students help children feel welcome in and attached to their schools.[130] To create such an environment, NASW believes it is necessary for schools to implement programs and curricula that require children to learn about tolerance of others at a very early age.[131]

Such programs are necessary to help students understand and deal with prejudice and differences among people, and are believed to be most effective if offered as soon as children begin kindergarten.[132] School systems have made strides in offering tolerance and diversity programs and students have responded.

Along the way, courts have been willing to protect these noble goals and honor their results.

For example, Massachusetts has a statute mandating the State Board of Education to establish standards that seek to eliminate gender, cultural, ethnic, and racial stereotypes, and requires students to understand differences in sexual orientation by the time they reach fifth grade.[133] This type of curriculum requirement is clearly supported by NASW's policy that children should receive an integrated education that "promotes understanding, knowledge, and acceptance of diversity in family composition (for example sexual orientation and same-sex families)."[134]

However, in *Parker v. Hurley*, parents of elementary school students brought suit against the Lexington, Massachusetts school district for its failure to provide prior notice that their elementary school children would be exposed to material promoting tolerance and understanding of gays and same-sex marriages.[135] The parents wanted notice, so that they would have the opportunity to "protect" their children from being subjected to books celebrating gay marriage and portraying families in which parents were of the same gender.[136]

The parents alleged that the school district was indoctrinating their children in beliefs that were contrary to their religious beliefs.[137] The Supreme Court essentially found that, because schools do not require students to read (or have read to them) books depicting or endorsing homosexuality, and do not require students to affirm those ideas, school districts can continue to expose children to books that encourage tolerance of gay people.[138]

Elsewhere, when a group of students seemed to have responded positively to the call to tolerance toward gays, school authorities tried to quash the students' efforts. The American Civil Liberties Union (ACLU) recently brought suit against a Florida high school that had been suppressing the First Amendment rights of students, gay and straight alike, to express support for equal rights for gay people.[139] The ACLU alleged that school officials routinely intimidated the plaintiff, along with other students, because she openly expressed her support for gay students.[140]

The students were in the practice of writing "gay pride" on their arms and notebooks, as well as wearing "rainbow-themed clothing."[141] The school's principal apparently admitted, during the trial, that he had banned students from expressing themselves in those ways, despite the fact that he continued to allow students to wear the divisive Confederate flag.[142] The ACLU reports that the Supreme Court enjoined the school from what was deemed to be the unconstitutional practice of censoring students who support the fair and equal treatment of gay people.[143] As avowed by the court, students "do not shed their constitutional rights to freedom of speech or expression at the schoolhouse gate."[144]

Right to Form Student Groups

In supporting efforts to improve LGBT people's status and well-being, NASW advocates for the right of lesbian and gay adolescents to develop supportive relationships with peers. NASW recognizes that groups like Gay-Straight Alliances (GSA) act as a safe harbor against the isolation of—and, often, discrimination against—gay and lesbian students in the educational process.[145] NASW promotes the idea that "lesbians and gays who have integrated a positive identity exhibit stronger psychological adjustment, greater satisfaction and higher self-concept, with lower rates of depression and stress."[146]

The Equal Access Act (EAA) provides that, whenever a public secondary school affords one or more noncurriculum related student groups the opportunity to meet on school grounds during noninstructional time, it must not preclude the noncurricular meetings of other students on the basis of "the religious, political, philosophical, or other content of the speech at such meetings."[147] In determining whether a student group has been denied equal access under EAA, the analysis necessarily turns to the meaning of "non-curriculum related student group." The Supreme Court has defined this term as: "any student group that does not *directly* relate to the body of courses offered by the school."[148]

If a school-sanctioned student group directly relates to a school's curriculum, the EAA is not implicated, and the school is not required to offer equal access to noncurriculum-related student groups.[149] Conversely, and most importantly, a school allowing noncurriculum-related student groups to meet must allow any other noncurriculum related student groups to meet.[150] However, the determination as to whether a particular student group is "non-curriculum related" depends on a given school's curriculum and is a question of fact that must be determined by trial courts on a case-by-case basis.[151]

In *Boyd County High School Gay Straight Alliance ("GSA") v. Board of Educ. of Boyd County*, the board sought to prevent a GSA student group from meeting at the school during noninstructional time by discontinuing the meetings of all curricular and noncurricular student groups.[152] The board was concerned about the disruption surrounding their prior decision to allow the GSA to meet.[153] Nonetheless, it permitted many other student groups to continue to meet during noninstructional time.[154]

The groups that continued to meet included the Bible Club, the Drama Club, the Beta Club, and the Executive Councils. All of these clubs were found by the Supreme Court to be unrelated to the particular curriculum of the Boyd County High School.[156] For instance, the purpose of the Executive Councils was to plan for the school's prom and ring selection.[157] Because those two purposes were found to be in no way related to the school's curriculum, the Board's actions of foreclosing the GSA's opportunity to meet were also held to be subject to EAA.[158]

It is worth noting that many schools have attempted to circumvent EAA protections by either alleging that GSA groups are a part of the school's already established curriculum, or by establishing a new curriculum that would include issues covered by GSA groups.[159] In *Colin ex rel. Colin v. Orange Unified School Dist.*, the Orange Unified School District's Board of Education denied students' application to form a GSA student group.[160] The board's own policy permitted noncurriculum-related student groups, and recognized that such groups have an important place in the lives of students.[161] However, the board sought to prevent the formation of the GSA by arguing that the group was related to the school's curriculum and therefore not protected by EAA.[162]

The board asserted that it had a curriculum in place that taught sex education, human sexuality, and sexual behavior through a combination of courses, such as health, biology, and family planning.[163] The GSA's proposed mission statement, though, indicated that the group did not intend to discuss what might be fairly called the "science of homosexuality"; rather, their focus would be issues concerning "tolerance" and "the need to treat everyone with respect."[164]

As such, the Supreme Court found as a matter of fact that the school's curriculum did not cover the proposed GSA's subject matter.[165] For the board to comply with EAA, it was found that the GSA must be permitted access to the school campus in the same manner that access was given to other noncurriculum student groups recognized by the school, such as the Christian Club and Key Club.[166]

It should also be noted that it is not unconstitutional for a public university to require students to pay an activities fee if the proceeds will ultimately help fund certain activities (e.g., an LGBT center).[167] As long as the school is viewpoint neutral in selecting what programs it will fund in an effort to facilitate extracurricular student speech, this is not a violation of the First Amendment.[168] So, there is at least a possibility that public secondary schools, which either welcome LGBT student groups or create conditions requiring the recognition of LGBT student groups (by allowing other noncurriculum student groups to exist), can also use student activities fees to fund LGBT group activities.

Protection from Harassment in Schools

Violence against LGBT students is prevalent in our school systems. At least one study has indicated that "45 percent of gay males and almost 20 percent of lesbians have experienced verbal abuse or physical assault in high school."[169] School officials may now be held liable for failing to put an end to the abuse and harassment of gay students.

In *Nabozny v. Podlesny*, a student who attended middle and high school in Wisconsin public schools was severely emotionally and physically abused at the hands of his classmates, over a period of several years.[170] The student was frequently beaten because he was openly gay. At one point, other male students held him down and subjected him to a mock rape.[171]

School officials seldom took sufficient action to protect him, and even responded, "Boys will be boys." Further, they insinuated that the student should expect such treatment for being openly gay.[172]

The student ultimately sued, and NASW filed an amicus brief, asserting that schools should be required to protect gay students, to mitigate the devastating effects of antigay violence.[173] The Supreme Court ultimately found that school officials could be held liable for discriminating against the student on the basis of his gender and/or his sexual orientation, in violation of the student's Fourteenth Amendment right to equal protection.[174]

Diversity in Schools

It is paramount to the proper education of children that an open and diverse learning environment is provided for them. It is NASW's policy that all children have a right to an equal educational opportunity that is integrated and "provide[s] for and facilitate[s] interaction among students and faculty of diverse racial, cultural, religious, spiritual, and ethnic backgrounds."[175]

Social workers are particularly well suited to help students and schools to fulfill this goal, as NASW seeks to promote cultural competency in social work practice.[176] NASW encourages the implementation of cultural and linguistic competency at the societal level, and charges social workers to help develop policies that "demand accountability of institutions."[177] To that end, NASW advocates for policies requiring cultural competency education, which is necessary to create a culturally diverse workforce.[178]

Although the focus of this law note is on the legal rights of primary and secondary school students, some positive gains have been made in promoting diversity at the postsecondary school level. Social workers can advocate that these gains be filtered down to the education of young children.

The Supreme Court decided two cases involving University of Michigan's undergraduate and law schools in the cases of *Gratz v. Bollinger*[179] and *Grutter v. Bollinger*,[180] respectively. The court reviewed the university's affirmative action policies, as applied to student admissions. In *Gratz*, University of Michigan undergraduate school ranked applicants on a 150-point scale, with 100 points being the score necessary for admission.[181] As part of its effort to achieve racial and ethnic diversity within its undergraduate student body, University of Michigan allocated an automatic 20-point bonus to underrepresented ethnic groups, such as Hispanics, Native Americans, and African Americans.[182] Two Caucasian applicants who were denied admission brought suit asserting a violation of the Equal Protection Clause of the Fourteenth Amendment.[183]

Whenever race-based classifications are used, the courts strictly scrutinize the constitutionality of the classifications under the Equal Protection Clause.[184] It must be demonstrated that the use of race is narrowly tailored to reach a compelling state interest.[185] The Supreme Court, in *Gratz*, conceded that educational diversity can constitute a compelling state interest. Nonetheless, it held that University of Michigan's undergraduate admissions policy was not narrowly tailored to achieve that interest, and therefore violated the Equal Protection Clause.[186]

The undergraduate admissions policy automatically gave underrepresented minorities 20 percent of the point total necessary for admission for no reason other than the very fact that they were underrepresented minorities.[187] This process was not narrowly tailored, because an applicant from an underrepresented group was automatically given a 20-point advantage in the admissions ranking process before receiving individual consideration.[188]

The University of Michigan law school also had an admissions policy that sought to achieve educational diversity. Unlike the undergraduate school's admissions policy, however, the law school admissions policy did not automatically assign points to underrepresented minorities. Rather, the law school admissions policy required that an applicant's entire file be reviewed, beyond grades and test scores, with consideration given to whether the applicant will help the law school achieve a diverse student body.[189] The admissions policy did not define the type of diversity sought, but it did make special reference to students from the same historically underrepresented groups outlined in the undergraduate admissions policy.[190]

In *Grutter*, the Supreme Court found that states do have a compelling interest in promoting diversity in higher education, if pursuing that interest focuses on race as only one of many factors for achieving a diverse student body. The law school's admissions policy was narrowly tailored to achieving educational diversity, since it was not aimed at filling any quota.[191] Instead, it was committed to conducting a highly individualized and comprehensive review of an applicant's file, "giving serious consideration to all the ways an applicant might contribute to a diverse educational environment."[192] As such, the law school's admissions policy did not violate the Equal Protection Clause.[193]

It may also be possible for primary and secondary public school systems to develop school districts with an eye toward achieving a diverse student population. The Supreme Court recently decided a case involving the issue of whether public school districts, on a voluntary basis, can use race to justify the selection and admission of students to public schools in the name of achieving diversity.[194] The school districts involved in this case were using the classifications "white and nonwhite" and "black or other" to determine to which schools students should be assigned.[195] The plurality opinion of the court found that state governments do not have a compelling interest in achieving diversity within public schools.[196]

Justice Kennedy's opinion, although concurring in the outcome, was more understanding of the goal of achieving diversity, and Kennedy's opinion likely carries great weight.[197] Agreeing with the plurality, Kennedy found that the school districts' diversity initiatives were too broad and imprecise, and that their use of race-based classifications to achieve diversity was arbitrary and inconsistent.[198]

Kennedy maintained, however, that schools do indeed have a compelling interest in achieving diversity and may continue to pursue the goal of achieving student bodies of diverse backgrounds through race-neutral means. Kennedy suggested that this may be done by:

- Creating school districts based on community demographics,
- Developing new schools in certain neighborhoods,
- Recruiting specific students and faculty, and
- Using statistics to track enrollments and performance by race.[199]

As such, the door is still open for school districts to pursue the goal of diversifying their student populations without violating constitutional standards.

Gender-Based Rights

Discrimination on the basis of gender has always been an area of concern for social workers. NASW is committed to advocating for affirmative action policies designed to level the playing field for groups, such as women, that were historically subjected to discrimination.[200] Curtailing gender-based discrimination begins by instilling in students notions of equality between the sexes through the advancement of equal educational opportunities. NASW recognizes that "the right to equal educational opportunity requires a non-segregated, nonsexist environment and a curriculum that reflects a pluralistic society."[201] The principal legal means for enforcing the equal treatment of male and female students is Title IX of the Education Amendments of 1972.

Title IX prohibits gender-based discrimination by mandating that, "No person in the United States shall, on the basis of sex, be excluded from participation in, be denied the benefits of, or be subjected to discrimination under any education program or activity receiving Federal financial assistance."[202] Because Title IX is a federal law, it only applies to institutions that receive federal funding.[203]

However, a great number of public and private school systems receive some sort of federal funding, so this requirement is not nearly as limiting as it may appear. If a school receives federal funding and fails to provide an equal educational opportunity pursuant to Title IX, it risks losing that funding. Nonetheless, school systems receiving federal funding have sought to limit the protections of Title IX in a number of creative ways.

Programs Subject to Title IX

School systems often have "independently" administered high school athletic programs. That is, schools may participate in athletic leagues or associations that are seemingly separate from the school systems, and that do not directly receive federal funding—even though the schools receive federal funding and pay the athletic leagues' membership fees. Given that federal funding is a necessary condition for requiring schools to provide equal education opportunities under Title IX, such arrangements can create problems when the athletic associations fail to provide equal opportunities for female students.

In *Horner v. Kentucky High School Athletics Ass'n (KHSAA)*, the Kentucky State Board for Elementary and Secondary Education managed and controlled all public schools for the Kentucky Department of Education.[204] The board designated KHSAA as its "agent," for purposes of managing the state's high school sports programs.[205] The Department of Education received substantial federal funds, but neither the Board nor KHSAA received direct federal funding.[206]

When the board and KHSAA were sued for violating Title IX, both entities defended by arguing that they did not have to comply with Title IX protections, because they were not themselves "recipients" of federal funds.[207] In examining the legislative history of Title IX and the federal regulations enacted pursuant to Title IX, the Supreme Court determined that, if any part of an agency receives federal funding, all entities within that agency must comply with Title IX protections.[208] Therefore, the court held that both the board and KHSAA could be found to be "recipients" of federal funding, by virtue of their position within the Kentucky Board of Education, which directly received federal funding.[209]

Conversely, the Supreme Court in *Johnny's Icehouse, Inc. v. Amateur Hockey Ass'n Illinois (AHAI), Inc.*, reached a very different conclusion in a case with facts similar to those in *Horner*. In *Johnny's Icehouse*, AHAI's members consisted of nearly every high school that fielded a hockey team.[210] Like KHSAA in the *Horner* case, AHAI did not directly receive federal funding.[211] AHAI member schools, which did receive federal funding, were required to pay membership fees.[212]

Ultimately, the Supreme Court found that Title IX did not apply to AHAI, because it was not a direct recipient of federal funding.[213] This case, however, may be distinguishable from *Horner* on the basis that AHAI was wholly independent from the member schools in Illinois, whereas KHSA was actually created as an agency for the benefit of the Kentucky Department of Education.

Substantive Protections of Title IX and Interscholastic Athletics

Historically, students have most often experienced gender-based discrimination in the area of interscholastic athletics. Being that interscholastic activities are an integral part of the education process, "discrimination in high school interscholastic athletics constitutes discrimination in education," and is controlled by Title IX.[214] A federal regulation enacted pursuant to Title IX provides that any recipient of federal funding that "operates or sponsors interscholastic, intercollegiate, club or intramural athletics shall provide equal athletic opportunity for members of both sexes."[215] It should be noted, however, that Title IX does not confer a right to participate in any given sport program, as there is no constitutional right to participate in high school athletics.[216]

Many instances of gender-based discrimination in interscholastic athletics center on the use of discriminatory scheduling schemes that effectively bar female students from full participation in sports of their choosing. In *McCormick ex rel. McCormick v. School Dist. of Mamaroneck*, two New York high schools fielded their girls' soccer teams during the spring semester of the school year, while the vast majority of New York schools fielded their girls' teams in the fall semester.[217] Because the regional and state championships for girls' soccer were held in the fall, female soccer players at the two high schools in question were effectively precluded from fully participating in their chosen sport.[218]

At the same two schools, the boys' soccer teams were fielded during the fall semester, and were able to compete for the regional and state championships.[219] As a result, the Supreme Court found that a disparity existed in treatment between the girls' and boys' soccer teams, which denied the girls equality of athletic opportunity under Title IX.[220] Similarly, in *Alston v. Virginia High School League, Inc.* (VHSL), the court found that participants in girls' interscholastic athletics have a Title IX claim where the VHSL scheduled girls' sports seasons differently from boys' sports seasons, which could effectively deprive girls of opportunities to play the sports of their preference.[221] Other areas of gender-based discrimination in interscholastic athletics focus on the appropriation of athletics equipment, facilities and practice times. In *Daniels v. School Bd. Of Brevard County, Fla.*, members of a girls' varsity softball team showed a substantial likelihood of success in a Title IX claim, as the team had not been provided many of the benefits provided to the boys' baseball team. These benefits included a lighted playing field, scoreboard, batting cage, superior bleachers, concessions, bathroom facilities, announcer's booth, and publicity for the games.[222]

Likewise, in *Ridgeway v. Montana High School Ass'n*, the Supreme Court found that female high school students were denied an equal education opportunity under Title IX, because girls' sports were underrepresented, underfunded, and discriminately scheduled. Furthermore, girls' teams were denied access to equally desirable facilities.[223] In remedying such disparities between girls' and boys' high school athletics programs, schools should improve girls' sports programs, rather than hindering boys' sports programs (e.g., by taking away any of the privileges enjoyed by a boys' sports team, such as access to better facilities).[224]

Issues Related to the School Environment

Harassment in Schools

The prevention of school violence has become a topic at the forefront of U.S. thought, following the multiple school shootings of the late 1990s. Although violent crime victimization in schools decreased between 1992 and 2001, according to the U.S. Department of Education and the U.S. Department of Justice, millions of children continue to be exposed to violence in their schools every year.[225] It is NASW's position that "all children have the right to attend a physically and emotionally safe school where they can maximize their academic potential."[226]

NASW policy supports schools' development of comprehensive violence prevention and intervention plans, which may even be required in some jurisdictions. Prevention initiatives help maintain school safety and enhance students' abilities to benefit from their educational experiences.[227] NASW "strongly supports the position that prevention initiatives are the most desirable for controlling and positively redirecting [violent] behaviors and they have the greatest long-term effect."[228] In this area, school social workers are "uniquely trained to identify students and families at risk, to provide diagnostic assessments, to understand the risk factors for individuals and families, to counsel students and families, and to arrange for referrals to appropriate community resources."[229]

An emerging issue concerning school violence is whether school districts and school officials may be held liable for their students' actions.[230] Initially, courts held that students do not possess a constitutional right to protection from the violence of other students by their school districts. However, victims of abuse or harassment have sought to hold school districts liable for abuse by a fellow student (i.e., peer sexual harassment) under three legal theories:

1. A federal law claim under Title IX of the Education Amendments of 1972,[231]
2. A federal civil rights claim under 42 U.S.C. § 1983,[232] and
3. An action for damages under applicable state laws.[233]

Title IX prohibits discrimination on the basis of sex in any federally funded education program.[234] Students can allege a violation of Title IX by arguing that being the victim of sexual harassment at school creates a hostile educational environment, which effectively bars the students' access to educational opportunities or benefits. Just as courts have found that employers create hostile work environments when they fail to stop sexual harassment between coworkers, school officials have been found to create a hostile educational environment when they fail to stop peer sexual harassment.[235]

It should be noted that courts initially refused to recognize a sexual harassment claim alleging a hostile educational environment under Title IX.[236] Yet, in 1992, the Supreme Court affirmed that students who are victims of sexual harassment at the hands of their teachers have an implied right of action under Title IX, when a school district that has been made aware of the alleged sexual harassment has taken no action.[237]

The Supreme Court also went one step further and held that monetary damages are an appropriate remedy for such an injury.[238] This decision paved the way for students who are victims of peer sexual harassment to be recognized. Parenthetically, it is necessary for social workers to remember that, while school districts may be held liable for damages stemming from student–teacher harassment, school social workers are still under a statutory duty to report any child abuse known to them.[239]

It is now settled that a school district may also be held liable for peer sexual harassment among students under certain circumstances.[240] In *Davis v. Monroe County Board of Education*,[241] the Supreme Court held that a school board may be liable in monetary damages under Title IX, if it was "deliberately indifferent" to the "severe and pervasive harassment," of which the board had "actual knowledge," when that harassment effectively barred the victim's access to an educational opportunity or benefit.[242]

Although this decision likely encourages school administrators to be more attuned to the possibility of peer sexual harassment among students, the Supreme Court left some crucial questions unanswered. These questions include:

1. What actions rise to the level of "severe and pervasive harassment"?
2. When does sexual harassment among students become "known" to the school district such that they must act?
3. How should school districts respond to sexual harassment claims so as to not be deemed "deliberately indifferent"?[243]

Alternatively, if a student has been abused or harassed by a peer, that student may be able to assert a Federal 42 U.S.C. Section 1983 claim against the school district. Section 1983 is a federal statute that provides a remedy to individuals who have been deprived of a constitutional or statutory right by the conduct of a state official, such as a school district or school officials.[244] Thus, school districts may be liable, under Section 1983, for the unconstitutional actions of their employees (e.g., if a school employee engages in sexual harassment of a student).

The issue of whether a school district is liable for the abusive or harassing behavior of one student toward another is less clear. One case in which a court determined that a school district might be found liable under Section 1983 was *Walton v. Alexander*.[245] In this case, a student at a residential school for the deaf sexually assaulted a classmate. The court held that, in a residential school situation, a "special custodial relationship" exists between the state official and the student, thus creating a constitutional right to protection and safety under Section 1983.[246]

Additionally, in *Murrell v. School District No. 1*,[247] the Tenth Circuit upheld a Section 1983 claim against a school district. The court ruled that a female student, who had properly alleged that school officials were deliberately indifferent toward the sexual harassment of a student by a peer, could maintain a claim against the school district.[248] However, courts have generally held that students do not possess a constitutional right to protection by a school district from abuse or harassment by individuals who are not school employees or officials—specifically, the acts of other students.[249]

Last, a school district may be liable under state tort law for the negligent supervision of the injured student, the abuser-student, or both. Although a determination of liability is based on multiple factors on a case-by-case basis, generally, a student must show that:

1. The school district had a duty to protect and supervise the students,
2. The school district breached that duty, and
3. The breach was the cause of the student's harm.[250]

As previously discussed, a school district may also be found liable to a student for peer sexual harassment under the state's civil rights statutes.[251] Further, as the legal system has begun to recognize that victims of peer sexual harassment do sometimes have a cause of action, school systems have responded by implementing policies aimed at stopping the harassment.[252] However, these policies do not alleviate the problem so much as they mitigate liability and the probability of successful lawsuits against schools.[253] To actually minimize peer sexual harassment, social workers can forge proactive and comprehensive interventions that "focus on the elimination of factors that contribute to a hostile school environment."[254]

Violence, generally, may be a significant part of the life experiences of young people, through personal encounters or through the media.[255] As noted in NASW's policy statement, *School Violence*, "chronic exposure to violence can adversely affect a child's ability to learn."[256] The U.S. Surgeon General's *Report on Youth Violence* states that violence prevention starts in the family and the community.[257] Because of their unique training, school social workers can play a major role in preventing school violence.

School social workers should have the opportunity to:

- Identify students at risk of violence, including bullying behavior in children, and victims of violence;

- Develop and implement school violence prevention programs, such as "character education programs, social skills training, conflict resolution programs, and peer mediation programs";

- Develop programs to strengthen family and parent relationships with the school;

- Develop programs to improve parenting skills; and

- Provide staff development programs, to teach staff about the prevalence and consequences of child and youth violence.[258]

School social workers can work with the school administration to implement comprehensive strategies for preventing and containing school violence, focusing on treatment of students, not just punishment.[259] This will serve the dual purposes of reducing the school's possible liability and enhancing the educational environment for all students.

Search and Seizure

Violence in schools has increased over the years, with national media focusing on guns and drugs in the schools and high profile incidents of violence. As a result, the courts have reviewed the issue of whether public- and private-school officials' have the right to search students, to protect the safety of the school environment.[260] The Fourth Amendment of the U.S. Constitution protects citizens from unwanted and unreasonable searches and seizures, particularly those conducted without a warrant.[261]

When warrantless searches are conducted in a school, usually by school officials, courts have balanced the students' constitutional rights with the social necessity of providing safe and effective schools. As noted by the Supreme Court in *Tinker v. Des Moines Independent Community School District*, "it can hardly be argued that either students or teachers shed their constitutional rights" when they enter into the school setting.[262] The court has further held that Fourth Amendment protection against unreasonable searches and seizures does not only apply to searches by law enforcement officers, but also by public school officials.[263]

When examining the question of a school's right to conduct a search, the courts first make a determination of whether a student has a reasonable expectation of privacy. Examples may include an expectation of privacy in the student's dormitory room,[264] the student's locker,[265] or the student's purse or backpack.[266] Courts then determine if the search was reasonable. The general rule in a school setting is that a search need not be based on probable cause but, rather, on "reasonableness."[267] According to the Supreme Court, in *New Jersey v. T.L.O.*, the search must be "justified at its inception," and "reasonably related in scope to the circumstances which justified the interference in the first place."[268]

Some courts have found exceptions to the general rule in various contexts. For example, courts have held that a search may be reasonable absent probable cause if there was individualized suspicion,[269] if the search was consented to by the student,[270] or if school officials had a "reasonable" suspicion.[271] Although jurisdictions differ on the reasonableness of searches, schools may adopt reasonable rules that allow school officials to search students or their possessions to protect school safety. Such rules should take into consideration applicable federal laws, state laws, and case interpretations that balance school safety with individual student rights.

Strip Searches

Perhaps not surprisingly, strip searching a student presents heightened privacy and practical concerns. In 2008, NASW filed an amicus brief in the case of *Redding v. Safford Unified School Dist. #1, et al.*,[272] which centered on the constitutionality of strip searches in schools. In *Redding*, a 13-year-old girl suspected of possessing prohibited ibuprofen was subjected to a strip search by the school nurse. The search was based solely on the word of a classmate, who had already been apprehended with the medication.[273]

The student brought suit, claiming that the school staff had violated her Fourth Amendment protections against unreasonable searches and seizures.[274] The Ninth Circuit Court of Appeals relied on the Supreme Court's decision in *T.L.O.* and applied a two-prong test for determining the constitutionality of the strip search.

First, the Ninth Circuit Court of Appeals found that the strip search of the young adolescent girl was unreasonable at the outset of the search because there was no credible information linking the young girl to the ibuprofen.[275] Second, the court found that the strip search did not reasonably relate to the objectives of the search, because the ibuprofen was not likely to be found in the girls' undergarments, given that prior searches of the girl's clothing and backpack yielded no results.[276]

The U.S. Supreme Court, which affirmed the unconstitutionality of the search, relied on NASW's amicus brief, and found that strip searches are inherently intrusive and can cause trauma and harm, especially to developing and self-conscious adolescents.[277] The Supreme Court cited social science findings presented by NASW that "strip search 'can result in serious emotional damage.'"

Given the wide evidence of trauma inflicted by strip searches, and the loss of trust of school personnel who conduct or condone them, school social workers should avoid involvement with such practices. Additionally, they should appropriately advocate for less intrusive, more positive disciplinary or investigative methods for students.

Drug Testing

As stated previously, if a state has undertaken to provide public education to its children, that education is a right that must be provided to all children on equal terms. However, the right to attend school is "the right to attend school subject to all lawful rules and regulations prescribed by the government" that are reasonably necessary to maintain order and discipline in the educational system.[278] Drug testing does constitute a search under the Fourth Amendment; however, a school district may create policies that require drug testing of students, if the testing is reasonably necessary to promote the safety of the school.[279]

Reasonableness of drug testing among students has been closely examined. For example the Supreme Court, in *Board of Education of Independent School District No. 92 of Pottawatomie County v. Earls*, determined that a school policy requiring all students participating in competitive extracurricular activities to take a drug test did not constitute an unreasonable search.[280] However, in other cases, courts have determined that school policies authorizing student drug testing have intruded on the legitimate expectation of privacy of the students.

For example, in *Tannahill ex rel. Lockney Independent School District*,[281] the Supreme Court held that a school district's mandatory drug testing policy for the entire school population was unreasonable and violated the students' Fourth Amendment rights.[282] Although jurisdictions differ on the breadth of drug testing permitted, students may be subjected to drug testing required by reasonable school policies aimed at protecting the safety of the school environment and promoting effective schools.

Student Dropouts

For schools, the problem of student dropouts is acute. High school dropout rates have remained the same or increased over the past 12 years, and the prospects for dropouts, as compared to high school graduates, are dim.[283] For students from low-income households, the dropout rate is as high as 10 percent. People in this dropout group face a higher-than-average unemployment rate (29.8 percent), a 3.5 times increased likelihood of being arrested over their lifetime, and an average income of $9,245 less than their high school graduate counterparts.

These effects are not just limited to the individual dropouts—high rates of dropout and poor education affect the entire country.[284]

School social workers should be involved in finding ways to keep students in school, to provide the education lawfully owed to every child in the United States. Identifying risk factors and influences at an early age can help school social workers and other school personnel to implement effective interventions.[285] School social workers are trained in assessing situations holistically, and can effectively advocate for increased resources for students, including:

- Bilingual education,
- Alternative schools,
- Fully staffed student service teams, and
- Recruitment of adult mentors.[286]

With these increased resources and interventions in place, school social workers can help students reach their potential and satisfy mandatory attendance laws.

Homeless Students

Another unique population that can assuredly be helped by school social workers is the growing population of homeless students. Homelessness, once thought to be an adult male problem, has seen increasing numbers of children and families over the last 25 years.[287] The 1990s were witness to a 3.5-fold increase in the number of children living in homelessness.[288] Throughout 2004, it was estimated that 1.35 million children were homeless, comprising 39 percent of the entire homeless population in the United States.[289]

In addition to increasing numbers of homeless students, significant academic disadvantages have been associated with homelessness.[290] The circumstances that lead to homelessness—such as poverty, child abuse and domestic violence, teen pregnancy, substance abuse, and lack of education for parents—are also associated with poor academic performance, regardless of whether or not the student is yet homeless.[291]

In addition, once becoming homeless, students face an increased chance of academic failure, because of barriers such as: frequent moving or changing of schools; lack of medical or personal records (e.g., birth certificate); the emotional trauma of losing friends and other attachments; lack of school supplies; poor health; and increased incidence of behavioral and emotional difficulties.[292] These factors all intersect to highlight the high-risk profile for this population.

These growing numbers, and the observed difficulties facing homeless students, demanded a legislative response from Congress. This response came in 2002, with the revised McKinney-Vento Education for Homeless Children and Youths

Act.[293] The McKinney-Vento Act provides a legal basis for the provision of special services for homeless students, to satisfy their right to a free and appropriate public education.[294] Congress, recognizing the unique challenges that homeless students face, sought to require and fund these services, in addition to prohibiting separation of homeless students from mainstream schools based solely on homelessness.[295] The act allocates funds to states to provide transportation, health services, social services, and special rights in school enrollment to homeless children.[296]

Great debate, however, has surfaced around the act. It has commonly been held to be grossly underfunded.[297] More strongly, though, the debate has centered around what essentially amounts to a prohibition on segregation of homeless students into homeless-only schools.[298] Proponents of segregation argue that mainstream schools will be unable to provide for the unique needs of homeless students, even with adequate funding.[299] They argue that, with adequate funding, separate, homeless-only schools are the only way to effectively educate homeless youth.[300]

Conversely, critics of homeless-only schools cite the poor accommodations of most homeless-only schools, and the lack of resources for special education and other unique needs.[301] Essentially, they claim that these schools are separate and unequal.[302] It is clear, however, from both sides, that greater conversation and resources need to be dedicated in service of the McKinney-Vento Act and the education of homeless children.

The provisions of the McKinney-Vento Act indicate a great need for school social workers' services. Social workers are in the unique position of managing homeless students' mental health, health, academic, and social service needs. Additionally, they can help provide the case management, referral networks, and advocacy necessary to help homeless students succeed.

Transporting Students in Private Vehicles

Policies on school employees transporting students in their personal vehicles vary from district to district. School social workers who are expected to carry out this function should be aware of the policy in their districts and schools. Rules on transport of students in private vehicles range from an outright ban to an allowance under certain conditions. These conditions may include a check of the social worker's driving record, assurance of the car's operable and safe condition, and specific insurance requirements. It is imperative that school social workers familiarize themselves with their schools' policies before agreeing to transport students in a personal vehicle.

In cases where social workers are permitted to transport students in their personal cars, several additional considerations must be taken into account. A social worker should explore the availability of insurance coverage in case of an accident. Some schools may have policies that provide for coverage for personal vehicles, but even those policies may require the initial exhaustion of one's personal policy limits.[303] Other schools may provide no insurance coverage, and require the employee's personal insurance to bear the full cost of liability. Additionally, some personal insurance policies may not cover commercial use of the vehicle. Therefore, checking with one's own insurance company may also be useful.

In addition to insurance, school employees should be aware of, and comply with, all local and state driving laws, including car- and booster-seat laws. Some states now require the use of booster seats for children up to eight years old, so many elementary school students will fall under this mandate.[304] School social workers who transport students in their personal vehicles should also clarify, ahead of time, the school's policy on reimbursement for gas and mileage to school activities.

Finally, the issue of permission is not to be overlooked. A school or district may have a particular administrator responsible for authorizing employees to transport students in their personal cars. The use of a parental permission slip is advisable, whether or not it is required.[305]

Issues Related to Social Work Services within the School

Parental Consent for Treatment

Generally speaking, parental consent is required for the medical treatment of a minor. However, this is not an absolute rule. Recognizing the importance of privacy around certain types of treatment for minors, states have created exceptions to this general rule. These exceptions can generally be broken into the following two broad categories:

1. Emancipated minors, and
2. Specific exemptions for unemancipated minors.[306]

Minors may be emancipated completely or for health care decisions.[307] These minors may consent to social work services in the same way that an adult could. Alternatively, unemancipated minors may be allowed to consent to treatment in specific circumstances and at certain ages.[308] Although this varies by state, there are some trends among the states.[309] Mental health treatment is one of these more common trends.[310] Individual states vary on the length or type of treatment for which minors may give consent. For example, some states allow minors above a certain age to consent to mental health treatment while limiting the number of sessions or requiring parental consent for medication.[311]

Consent to treatment is especially important in the realm of mental health and social work services, because the right to consent generally confers with it a right to confidentiality.[312] In a school setting, confidentiality is of special concern. Students may be unwilling or hesitant to disclose completely to a school social worker unless they can be assured that their communications will be kept confidential—even from their parents. One author found that most agencies and medical professionals that work with youth and adolescents believed they would not seek these services without a promise of confidentiality.[313] It is important, therefore, that school social workers familiarize themselves with the laws in their jurisdictions, to provide social work services in as confidential a manner as possible.

Confidentiality and Information Sharing

Confidentiality is particularly complex legal area for social workers working in education. Like others in the profession, school social workers are to be guided by the *NASW Code of Ethics* as a primary source for best practice principles. However, the layers of applicable federal, state, and local laws and regulations add areas of consideration that may complicate decision making in specific situations. This section discusses the various issues school social workers face when dealing with client confidentiality and information sharing.

Since the late 1960s, the Supreme Court has upheld U.S. citizens' constitutionally protected right to privacy.[314] From the early cases of *Griswold v. Connecticut* and *Roe v. Wade*, the court has firmly held that certain rights of privacy are protected from government interference under the Due Process Clause of the Fourteenth Amendment.[315] However, there are limits to these constitutionally protected rights. An individual's federal constitutional rights are only invoked when there is federal or state government action. Thus, people may only make valid constitutional arguments if they are "challenging a state statute or when the breach of confidentiality occurs in a case involving a governmental agency," including public schools and the offices that administer them.[316]

NASW Code of Ethics, Section 1.07, Privacy and Confidentiality

Section 1.07(a), Privacy and Confidentiality, of the *NASW Code of Ethics* states that, "social workers should respect clients' right to privacy."[317] The social worker has an obligation not to seek personal information from a client, unless the information is vital to "providing services or conducting social work evaluation or research."[318] Furthermore, if the client shares any private information with the social worker, the "standards of confidentiality apply."[319]

A preliminary question for school social workers, when faced with the issue of confidentiality, is: "Who is the client?" Ultimately, the student is the most important client. Services may also be provided, however, to family members, staff, and administration, in furtherance of a student's social and educational goals.

According to the U.S. Census Bureau, 68,698,000 students were enrolled in school in 2000, with a projected 71,794,000 enrolled in 2005.[320] School social workers are responsible for "helping students make satisfactory school adjustments and coordinating and influencing the efforts of the school, the family, and the community to help achieve this goal."[321]

Problems may arise when school social workers consider the students, their parents, school administrators, teachers, and the community as equal clients.[322] Although it is true that all of these parties have a stake in the child's education and life, giving equal consideration to all of the parties forces the social worker to juggle their competing interests.[323] The social worker must determine if the stakeholders' desire to have confidential information about a child is synonymous with "their right to know such information."[324]

Confidentiality and Information Sharing with Parents

The confidentiality of a student or minor's school and mental health records creates special issues for school social workers. On the basis of various state laws, a minor or child is a person who is under the age of majority.[325] Until the minor attains the age of majority, or is emancipated by a legally recognized event,[326] the parents or legal guardians are generally entitled to access their confidential information. One text explains that the legal rights of children "should be viewed as a continuum." Infants are generally given the least amount of rights, and their parents have virtually absolute authority over decisions affecting their lives. However, as minors reach adolescence, parental authority lessens and the minors are given greater rights.[327]

It is the school social worker's responsibility to adhere to the wishes of the parent or guardian, as well as those of the child. The Family Educational Records Protection Act (FERPA)[328] guarantees parents' free access to student school records. Under FERPA, federal funds can be withheld from education agencies or institutions that do not make these records available to parents or legal guardians. This act not only ensures parents' access to their child's school records, but also protects individuals' rights to the privacy of such records.

Thus, on the basis of federal law, a school social worker generally would not be able to withhold information in a student's educational record from a parent, if that information may help them make an informed decision concerning their child's care. However, the issue of whether the school social worker's file is a part of a student's school record may be unclear, and may rest on an analysis of a number of factors, including:

1. Whether the social worker is an employee of the school system, and thereby subject to the school system's rules and regulations;
2. Whether the social worker is an independent contractor; or
3. Whether the school or social worker have written policies and procedures to be followed, and whether they are based on state law.

Parents' rights and authority over their children are limited as their children approach the age of majority. Older teenagers' rights of privacy "parallel those of adults, with the same recognized exceptions for harm to life."[329] The school social worker will ordinarily protect a student's rights, to provide effective counseling. In protecting these rights, the school social worker must take into consideration ethical obligations, the student's best interest, and state and local law. In most situations, adolescents should be encouraged to inform their parents themselves about matters that parents need to know.[330] In addition, a child or teenager should be informed about: (1) the type of information that will be shared with the parents, and (2) that which can be kept in confidence.[331]

In some situations, sustaining confidentiality is not in the best interests of the child. The *NASW Code of Ethics* notes that confidentiality should be protected by the social worker during the course of providing professional services. However, if there are "compelling professional reasons" to disclose such information, then the social worker may do so.[332] The general rule is that the social worker should disclose "the least amount of confidential information to achieve the desired purpose."[333] Also, information that is revealed should be directly linked to the purpose of the disclosure.[334]

Confidentiality Dilemmas

There are several situations in which the decision of whether or not to disclose confidential information is cloudier. Broadly, these dilemmas arise around four main issues:

1. A student's potential harm to self,
2. A student's potential harm to others,
3. Another's harm to the student, and
4. The student's reproductive rights.

Situations involving a student's potential harm to him or herself may include any of a number of self-destructive behaviors. It is almost always appropriate and prudent in these situations for the social worker to inform the minor student's parents. Three prevalent self-harming behaviors or threatened self-harming behaviors that may be brought to a school social worker's attention are: self-injury, eating disorders, and suicidal threats.

The most dramatic and serious of these behaviors—suicide—is of special concern to school social workers. Because of their regular contact with the student, school personnel may be in the best position (along with the family) to identify and prevent teen and youth suicide.[335] School social workers' specific training and ability to identify and distinguish suicidal behavior and gestures places them in a position to create, implement, and advocate for suicide prevention programs—on a schoolwide level for all students, and on a personal level for at-risk students.[336] By taking on this leadership role in suicide prevention, school social workers can ensure the implementation of valid and comprehensive interventions.[337]

In addition to dilemmas involving self-harm, a school social worker may also be faced with the dilemma of one student's threatened harm to another. After the landmark case of *Tarasoff v. Regents of the Univ. of California*, many states adopted "duty to warn" statutes, imposing an affirmative duty on mental health professionals to report any imminent risk of serious harm from a patient to law enforcement and/or the intended victims.[338] In often-complicated situations, school social workers may be forced to determine the extent or imminence of a client's threat, balancing the various and multiple risks to public welfare with the risk involved in breaching the student's confidentiality.[339]

The issue of confidentiality breaches for school social workers in cases of danger of harm to others is also governed by the Federal Educational Rights and Privacy Act.[340] FERPA generally requires that schools may not release student information without parental consent.[341] FERPA, however, does include an exception for "health and safety emergencies."[342] Under these circumstances, school personnel may release otherwise confidential information to "protect the health and safety of the student or other individuals."[343]

School social workers who receive confidential information from students in the course of their work should similarly be able to release it during health and safety emergencies, without risking their ethical and legal obligations of confidentiality.[344] This exception is limited, however, to appropriate parties and to the time of the emergency.[345] Further, it does not permit the disclosure of any of the minor student's treatment records whose protection is governed by state law.[346]

A third area in which breaching confidentiality is appropriate is suspected or reported child abuse or school bullying. Whenever potential sexual or physical abuse of a minor comes to a social worker's attention, she or he is bound by law and ethics to report such behavior to the proper authorities. The 1974 Child Abuse Prevention and Treatment Act (CAPTA) distributes federal funds to the states "in support of prevention, assessment, investigation, prosecution, and treatment activities related to child abuse and neglect."[347] CAPTA stipulated that states had to create a system for reporting child abuse to receive the federal funds promised in the act. Today, all states have designated social workers as mandated reporters.

It is important to point out that social workers may encounter situations where the issue is not whether the sexual abuse should be reported, but whether it should be disclosed. There is little doubt that a student who shares his or her sexual abuse history with a social worker in a treatment setting has a constitutional right of privacy requiring the student's communications to remain confidential.[348] However, at least one court has determined that this right is not violated when a social worker discloses it in a professional setting, to further the student's interests. The U.S. District Court for the Southern District of New York found that a student's right of confidentiality is not breached when a social worker discloses the student's sexual abuse history as part of an evaluation aimed at classifying the student as "emotionally disturbed" for purposes of obtaining special education under IDEA.[349]

School social workers are also often confronted with students who have been physically and emotionally victimized by school bullies. Issues of confidentiality arise when a student seeking counseling from a school social worker requests that the social worker not reveal the names of the school bullies, out of fear of retribution. For instance, Illinois, like most states, proscribes the disclosure of confidential communications made to social workers.[350] There are, however, exceptions that allow disclosure in certain instances. One such instance might be when, in the social worker's sole discretion, she or he determines that disclosure is necessary to protect the client from physical or mental harm.[351]

The Appellate Court of Illinois found that this exception protects social workers who disclose the identity of school bullies to school officials, even when a student and her or his parents explicitly request that the identities not be disclosed.[352] The school social worker has broad discretion when evaluating whether that type of disclosure is needed to protect the student from a continuing threat of abuse from bullies.[353] Furthermore, the social worker's disclosure is presumed to be in good faith, even if the student or the student's parents did not endorse the disclosure.[354] Under the Illinois court's ruling, a social worker who tricks a student into revealing the names of bullies by promising not to disclose may still be considered to have acted in good faith if that social worker believes disclosure is necessary to prevent future bullying.[355]

Finally, school social workers may face a dilemma when confronted with a minor student who is seeking advice or support surrounding reproductive rights. At what age a student may seek an abortion without parental consent as well as whether or not a social worker may refer a minor student to Planned Parenthood, for example, with or without informing her parents are important and relevant questions to the practice of school social work. The issue of parental notification regarding a minor student's pregnancy has been reviewed by the New York courts in *Port Washington Teachers' Assoc. v. Bd. of Educ. Of the Port Washington Union Free Sch. Dist.*[356] In that case, a teachers' union and a school social worker brought suit to bar a policy that required them to report student pregnancies.[357] In its amicus brief for the teachers' association, the ACLU referenced many leading medical organizations that opposed parental notification because of the resulting resistance to care.[358]

Other justifications have been offered in opposition to requiring school personnel to notify parents of student pregnancies—both practical and more theoretical. For example, many states have statutes allowing pregnant teens to consent to prenatal medical care and medical care for their child.[359] It seems, therefore, in opposition to the teen's right to consent to treatment to not allow her to consent to an abortion. Beyond these theoretical conflicts, there are also practical and realistic concerns to requiring parental consent for an abortion. Some authors express concern over a veto right to abortion for parents or other third parties, which essentially renders the student's right to an abortion futile.[360] Further, concerns about student safety and potential abuse or other domestic problems reiterate the point that the student, not the social worker or other school personnel, is best suited to determine when and if to tell her parents.[361]

Conclusion

School social workers' ability to provide high quality professional services to students will be enhanced by their knowledge of the legal framework in which they practice. The legal rights and obligations of a school system, its employees, the students, and their families often overlap, and may create ethical dilemmas for school social workers. An awareness of the potential legal issues will assist social workers in their professional and ethical decision-making processes.

Social workers contemplating a career in the schools should have a clear understanding of the credentialing and licensing requirements in their state, taking care to review both social work licensing board standards and any applicable standards of the state's education department. Those contemplating the possibility of relocating to another state should carefully evaluate any specialized certification or licensing requirements in the new jurisdiction, and should plan to address potential barriers in advance.

Social workers' roles are varied within the school system and an understanding of students' legal rights in specific situations may be useful to address key issues. These issues include students' rights to access the educational system, regardless of ethnic, racial, and other differences, as well as parents' rights to make choices about their children's education.

In addition to the long-standing legal issues related to racial and ethnic diversity in the schools, and equal treatment regardless of race and gender, other issues may confront students. These may include:

- Access to special education services,

- Education for learners whose primary language is not English,

- Freedom from harassment for gay, lesbian, bisexual, and transgender students, or

- Services for homeless students.

Students may face an array of school rules and approaches to enforcement, including random drug testing, searches of lockers and of the person, and notification of parents. Many of these policies and practices are rooted in the schools' obligations to maintain a safe and secure learning environment. Social workers' ability to maintain professional confidentiality standards and to exercise professional discretion about the disclosure of students' private information may conflict with school system policies or parental expectations—particularly with regard to illegal or potentially dangerous behavior. Astute school social workers will seek clarification in advance of school system policies regarding consent to treatment, parental notification, and any mandatory disclosures of student information. They may then seek to resolve any potential conflicts with social work standards.

School social work practice presents many opportunities for professional satisfaction, along with challenges such as those discussed above. School social workers are positioned at the cutting edge of many legal issues facing adolescents. They have, therefore, a unique opportunity to promote the recognition of social work values as they advocate for students and their families.

Appendix A

School Social Worker Statutes

As the range of services provided by school social workers has expanded, regulation of the practice of school social work has become more prevalent. In regulating the profession, states have taken several different actions. Many states have separate licensing or credentialing requirements for school social workers; some states require school social workers to be certified by NASW; and most states have standards that must be followed, for school social workers to provide services to schools within their jurisdiction.

The following chart provides a state-by-state summary of state statutes and regulations outlining the requirements for school social worker certification. Column 2 lists the relevant state laws governing the certification of school social workers. Column 3 provides the language of the applicable provisions of the statutes listed in Column 2. Column 4 provides exemptions that may apply to school social workers (or social work students), which may excuse them from having to obtain licensure from the state social work licensing board while practicing in the schools. It is important to note that use of the phrase "No Exemption" under Column 4 does not exempt school social workers from the requirements found in Column 3.

APPENDIX A: School Social Worker Statutes

State	School Social Worker Certification Relevant Statute	Relevant Text	State(s) "Professional" Licensing Boards Exemption for Social Work Licensure
Alabama	No specific provision with regards to certification requirements for School Social Workers.		No exemption from social work licensing requirements

State	School Social Worker Certification Relevant Statute	Relevant Text	State(s) "Professional" Licensing Boards Exemption for Social Work Licensure
Alaska	ALASKA ADMIN. CODE tit. 4 §12.365 (2005) ALASKA ADMIN. CODE tit. 4 §12.305 (2005) ALASKA ADMIN. CODE tit. 4 §12.355 (2005)	§ 12.365. Certification for related services providers. A person employed to provide related services as defined in 4 AAC 52.990 ... including ... social work ... must possess a (1) teacher certificated issued under 4 AAC 12.305 endorsed in the field of employment; or (2) special services certificate (Type C) issued under 4 AAC 12.355 in the field of employment. § 12.305. Teacher certificate (initial, professional, master). (a) Except as provided in AS 14.20, the department will issue an initial teacher certificate, valid for up to three years under (d) of this section, to an applicant who (1) has satisfied the baccalaureate degree requirement of AS 14.20.020 ... (b) The department will issue a professional Teacher certificate, valid for five years to an applicant who has (1) met the requirements of (a) of this section for an initial teacher certificate; (2) passed (A) the competency examination by achieving qualifying scores as described in (a)(2) of this section, if under AS 14.20.015, qualifying scores as described in (a)(2) of this section ... (3) Complete three semester hours in Alaska studies and three semester hours in multicultural education or cross cultural communications ... § 12.355. Special services certificate (Type C): provisional certificate (provisional Type C). (a) The department will issue a special services certificate (Type C), valid for five years, to an applicant who has completed a program in a special service area, has a bachelor's or higher degree, and is recommended by the preparing institution. (b) Except as otherwise provided in this chapter, the applicant must have earned at least six semester hours of credit within the five years immediately preceding application ... (e) To meet the requirements of (a) of this section, the applicant must have satisfactorily completed three semester hours in Alaska studies and three semester hours in multicultural education or cross-cultural communication ...	No exemption from social work licensing requirements
Arizona	No specific provision with regards to certification requirements for School Social Workers.		No exemption from social work licensing requirements

State	School Social Worker Certification Relevant Statute	Relevant Text	State(s) "Professional" Licensing Boards Exemption for Social Work Licensure
Arkansas	016–06–053 ARK. CODE R. § 201.000 (2001) 016–06–053 ARK. CODE R. § 202.100 (2001)	201.000 Introduction — In order to ensure quality and continuity of care, school districts and/or Education Services Cooperatives (ESC) that are providers of School-Based Mental Health Services, approved to receive Medicaid reimbursement for services provided to the under age 21 Medicaid population, must ensure that contractors and personnel engaged as licensed school-based mental health practitioners meet specific qualifications in order for school districts and ESC providers to bill Medicaid for their services. 202.100 Requirements for Certification of Provider Staff or Contracted Professionals Who Provide School-Based Mental Health Services. School district and Educational Services Cooperative (ESC) mental health provider employee and contractor requirements are as follows: A. Licensed Certified Social Worker (LCSW) 1. The LCSW must possess a master's degree in social work from a graduate school of social work accredited by the Council on Social Work Education (CSWE). 2. The LCSW must be state licensed and certified to practice as a licensed certified social worker in the State of Arkansas and in good standing with the Arkansas Social Work Licensing Board. 3. The LCSW must provide to the school district or ESC proof of two years post licensure experience treating children and adolescents with mental illness. 4. The LCSW shall not provide services beyond those for which he or she has been trained and are within his or her scope of practice and licensure. NOTE: A licensed certified social worker employed or contracted with the school district or ESC may not be enrolled in the Targeted Case Management (TCM) Program. He or she must choose only one of those programs in which to participate. B. Licensed Master Social Worker (LMSW) 1. The LMSW must have a master's degree from an accredited social work program in an accredited institution approved by the Council on Social Work Education (CSWE). 2. The LMSW must be state licensed and certified to practice as a licensed master social worker in the State of Arkansas and in good standing with the Arkansas Social Work Licensing Board. 3. The LMSW must work under the supervision of an LCSW. 4. The LMSW shall not provide services beyond those for which he or she has been trained and are within his or her scope of practice and licensure. 5. The LMSW shall not provide services beyond those for which he or she has been trained and are within his or her scope of practice and licensure. NOTE: A licensed certified social worker employed or contracted with the school district or ESC may not be enrolled in the Targeted Case Management (TCM) Program. He or she must choose only one of those programs in which to participate.	No exemption from social work licensing requirements

State	School Social Worker Certification Relevant Statute	Relevant Text	State(s) "Professional" Licensing Boards Exemption for Social Work Licensure
California	Cal. Educ. Code § 44874 (2006) Cal. Educ. Code § 44267 (2006)	§ 44874. Qualifications for psychologist or social worker. The qualifications for a psychologist or social worker are a valid certificate issued by the appropriate California agency authorized by law to certify such persons and a services credential with a specialization in health. Any school district may employ and compensate psychologists and social workers meeting the foregoing qualifications. § 44267. Services credential with specialization in health. The minimum requirements for a services credential with a specialization in health are: (a) Five years, or its equivalent, of college or university education, or five years of professional preparation approved by the commission. (b) Possession of a valid license, certificate, or registration, appropriate to the health service to be designated, issued by the California agency authorized by law to license, certificate, or register persons to practice that health service in California.	See Cal. Bus. & Prof. Code § 4996.14 (2003) Employees working under the supervision of an employer that is (1) A governmental entity; (2) A school, college, or university; (3) An institution that is both nonprofit and charitable.
Colorado	Colo. Rev. Stat. § 12–43–408 (2003)	§ 12–43–408. School social workers. Any person who holds a valid master's degree in social work and has obtained the special services license with social work endorsement issued by the department of education pursuant to the "Colorado Educator Licensing Act of 1991", article 60.5 of title 22, C.R.S., shall be issued the "LISW" certificate upon application and payment of said fees and shall be subject to the provisions of this article. (See also, Colo. Rev. Stat. § 22–60.5–210. Types of special services licenses issued — term.)	No exemption from social work licensing requirements
Connecticut	Conn. Agencies Regs. § 10.145D-564 (1993) Conn. Agencies Regs. § 10.145D-566 (1993)	§ 10–145d-564. Initial educator certificate requirements. To receive an initial educator certificate to serve as a school social worker, the applicant shall meet the following requirements, in addition to meeting the assessment requirements, as appropriate: (a) Holds a mater's degree in social work from a school of social work accredited by the Council on Social Work Education, and (b) Has completed a course of study in special education comprised of not fewer than 36 clock hours, which shall include study in understanding the growth and development of exceptional children, including handicapped and gifted and talented children and children who may require special education, and methods for identifying, planning for and working effectively with special-needs children in the regular classroom. (See also Conn. Agencies Regs § 10–145–565. Provisional educator certificate requirements). §10–145d-566. Professional educator certificate requirements. To receive a professional educator certificate for school social worker an applicant shall present evidence of 30 school months of successful service under the provisional educator certificate, interim provisional educator certificate, or provisional teaching certificate.	No exemption from social work licensing requirements

State	School Social Worker Certification Relevant Statute	Relevant Text	State(s) "Professional" Licensing Boards Exemption for Social Work Licensure
Delaware	Del. Code Ann. tit. 14 § 1582 (1994)	PART 1582 STANDARD CERTIFICATE SCHOOL SOCIAL WORKER Section 3.0 Standard Certificate. In accordance with 14 Del.C. §1220(a), the Department shall issue a Standard Certificate as a School Social Worker to an applicant who holds a valid Delaware Initial, Continuing, or Advanced License; or Standard or Professional Status Certificate issued by the Department prior to August 31, 2003, and who meets the following requirements. 3.1 Master's Degree School Social Worker (MSW) 3.1.1 Master's degree in Social Work (MSW) from a regionally accredited college or university and, 3.1.2 Two years successful full time work experience as a social worker, and 3.1.3 One year of supervised experience in a school setting, or a ono year internship of 1000 hours approved by the Department of Education and supervised by an approprlate school designee.	No exemption from social work licensing requirements

State	School Social Worker Certification Relevant Statute	Relevant Text	State(s) "Professional" Licensing Boards Exemption for Social Work Licensure
District of Columbia	D.C. Mun. Regs. tit. 5, § 1660 (1993)	§ 1660. School Social Worker. 1660.1 For certification as a school worker, the following shall be required: (a) A master's degree in social work from an accredited institution of social work that includes the following: *(1)* Field practicum in a setting providing direct services to individuals and groups of school age children and their families; or *(2)* A minimum of one (1) year paid professional experience (post master's degree) in a setting providing direct services to individuals and groups of school age children and their families; (b) Program content to include the following: *(1)* Four (4) semester hours in family and child related coursework; *(2)* Four (4) semester hours in human behavior and social environment; *(3)* Four (4) semester hours in social welfare policy and services; *(4)* Eight (8) semester hours in social work practice; *(5)* Four (4) semester hours in research; and *(6)* Six (6) semester hours to include the following: *(A)* Laws and regulations, which impact upon school programs; and *(B)* Content in the area of disabling conditions and appropriate interventions; (c) Skills to include the following: *(1)* Developing a social history and psychological assessments by use of appropriate methodologies and theories (i.e., systems, family psychological theories and framework); *(2)* Utilizing theoretical and practice knowledge in counseling (i.e., family dynamics, crisis intervention and mediation); *(3)* Communication (i.e., speech, writing, sign language when/where appropriate); *(4)* Child and adolescent development theories (i.e., typical vs. atypical development; life cycle issues); *(5)* Learning and behavioral theories; *(6)* The influence of situations which impact upon individuals, families, and communities; *(7)* Law and legal provisions in the area of child welfare; *(8)* The cause and effects of social, cultural, and environmental forces and their impact on learning and human behavior (i.e., effect of these forces on race, ethics, gender, socio-economic status); and *(9)* The role and function of the school social worker in relationship to school, communities, and organizations; and (d) A valid license to practice social work in the District of Columbia.	No exemption from social work licensing requirements
Florida	Fla. Admin. Code Ann. r. 6A-4.035 (1996)	§ 6A-4.035. Specialization Requirements for Certification in School Social Worker (Grades PK-12)—Specialty Class. A bachelor's or higher degree with an undergraduate or graduate major in social work. The program shall be accredited by the nation al Council on Social Work Education or the institution shall be accredited in accordance with the provisions of Rule 6A-4.003, FAC.	No exemption from social work licensing requirements

State	School Social Worker Certification Relevant Statute	Relevant Text	State(s) "Professional" Licensing Boards Exemption for Social Work Licensure
Georgia	GA. COMP. R. & REGS. 505–2–0.205 (2006)	§ 505–2-.205. School Social Work. (1) Certificate Requirements. (c) Non-Renewable Professional Certificate (See Rule 505–2-.06); *1.* If the applicant currently holds a Clear Renewable Certificate in any field, a Non-Renewable Certificate in this field may be issued at the request of an employing school system based on verification of acceptance into either a state-approved School Social Work program OR a PSC-approved accredited Master's of Social Work (M.S.W.) degree program; *2.* If the applicant holds a valid or expired professional out-of-state certificate in School Social Work and the highest degree held is a bachelor's degree in Social Work, the certificate will be issued as a Non-Renewable Professional Certificate to allow time for completion of a state-approved master's degree program in School Social Work or a PSC-approved accredited Master's of Social Work (M.S.W.) degree program and Special Georgia Requirements. *3.* If the applicant holds a bachelor's degree in Social Work AND has passed the Basic Skills Assessment, the certificate will be issued as a Non-Renewable Professional Certificate to allow time for completion of either a state-approved master's degree program in School Social Work or a PSC-approved accredited Master's of Social Work (M.S.W.) degree program and completion of Special Georgia Requirements. *4.* If the applicant holds an expired Level 5 Georgia School Social Work certificate, a Non-Renewable Certificate in this field may be issued at the request of an employing school system to satisfy Special Georgia Requirements. If the expired Georgia School Social Work certificate is Level 4, the applicant must complete a state-approved master's degree program in School Social Work or a PSC-approved accredited Master's of Social Work (M.S.W.) degree program and applicable Special Georgia Requirements.	*See* GA. CODE ANN. § 43–10A-7 (2003) Employee of any agency or department of the state or any of its political subdivisions Employee of any agency or department of the state or any of its political subdivisions to provide services to persons with disabilities Student interns — also professional counselors and marriage and family therapy interns School counselors Limited licensure for CSWE bachelors graduates Counselor with University System of Georgia
Hawaii	No specific provision with regards to certification requirements for School Social Workers.		

State	School Social Worker Certification Relevant Statute	Relevant Text	State(s) "Professional" Licensing Boards Exemption for Social Work Licensure
Idaho	IDAHO ADMIN. CODE R. 08.02.02.027 (2004)	§ 027. PUPIL PERSONNEL SERVICES CERTIFICATE. 07. School Social Worker Endorsement. This endorsement is valid for five (5) years. Six (6) credit hours are required every five (5) years in order to renew the endorsement. Initial endorsement may be accomplished through possession of a social work certificate issued by the Idaho Bureau of Occupational Licenses, an institutional recommendation, and completion of one (1) of the following options: (3–16–04) a. A master's degree in social work from an Idaho college or university approved by the State Board of Education, or a master's degree in social work from an out-of-state college or university. The program must be currently approved by the state educational agency of the state in which the program was completed. (3–16–04) b. A master's degree in guidance and counseling, sociology, or psychology plus thirty (30) semester credit hours of graduate work in social work education, including course work in all the following areas: understanding the individual; casework method; field placement; social welfare programs and community resources; and research methods. (3–16–04)	No exemption from social work licensing requirements
Illinois	105 ILL. COMP. STAT. 5/14–1.09A (1990)	§ 5/14–1.09a. School social worker. "School Social Worker" means a social worker who has graduated with a master's or higher degree in social work from an accredited graduate school of social work and who has such additional qualifications as may be required by the State Board of Education and who holds a School Service Personnel Certificate endorsed for school social work issued pursuant to Section 21–25 of this Code. Persons so certified may use the title "school social worker" and may offer school social work services which are limited to those services set forth in 23 Ill. Adm. Code 226, Special Education, pertaining to children between the ages of 3 to 21, promulgated by the State Board of Education. School social workers may make evaluations, recommendations, or interventions regarding the placement of children in educational programs or special education classes. However, a school social worker shall not provide such services outside his or her employment to any student in the district or districts which employ such school social worker.	225 ILL. COMP. STAT. 20/4 (1995) Employed by the United States government or by the State of Illinois, unit of local government or any bureau, division or agency thereof Social work student
Indiana	IND. CODE ANN. § 20–20–19–1 (2001)	§ 20–20–19–1 Qualifications. Sec. 1. (a) An individual who obtains a position as a school social worker for a school corporation must: (1) hold a master's degree in social work; or (2) agree as a condition of employment to obtain a master's degree in social work not more than five (5) years after the individual begins employment as a school social worker. (b) Subsection (a) does not apply to an individual who obtained a position as a school social worker for a school corporation before July 1, 2001.	No exemption from social work licensing requirements

State	School Social Worker Certification Relevant Statute	Relevant Text	State(s) "Professional" Licensing Boards Exemption for Social Work Licensure
Iowa	Iowa Admin. Code r. 285–15.19 (1992)	282–15.19(272) School social worker. 15.19(1) *Authorization.* An individual who meets the requirements of subrule 15.19(2) or 15.19(3) is authorized to serve as a school social worker to pupils from birth to age 21 (and to a maximum allowable age in accordance with Iowa Code section 256B.8). 15.19(2) *Option 1: Endorsement requirements.* An applicant must hold a master's degree in social work from an accredited school of social work to include a minimum of 20 semester hours of coursework (including practicum experience) which demonstrates skills, knowledge, and competencies in the following areas: a. Social work. (1) Assessment (e.g., social, emotional, behavioral, and familial). (2) Intervention (e.g., individual, group, and family counseling). (3) Related studies (e.g., community resource coordination, multidiscipline teaming, organizational behavior, and research). b. Education. (1) General education (e.g., school law, foundations of education, methods, psycho-educational measurement, behavior management, child development). (2) Special education (e.g., exceptional children, psycho-educational measurement, behavior management, special education regulations, counseling school-age children). c. Practicum experience. A practicum experience in a school setting under the supervision of an experienced school social work practitioner is required. The practicum shall include experiences that lead to the development of professional identity and the disciplined use of self. These experiences will include: assessment, direct services to children and families, consultation, staffing, community liaison and documentation. If a person has served two years as a school social worker, the practicum experience can be waived. d. Completion of an approved human relations component is required. e. The program must include preparation that contributes to the education of students with disabilities and students who are gifted and talented. 15.19(3) *Option 2: Statement of professional recognition (SPR).* The special education director (or designee) of the area education agency or local education agency must submit an application to request that the authorization be issued. The application must include: a. An official transcript that reflects the master's degree in social work; and b. The licensed independent social worker (LISW) or licensed master social worker (LMSW) license issued by the Iowa board of social work examiners.	No exemption from social work licensing requirements

State	School Social Worker Certification Relevant Statute	Relevant Text	State(s) "Professional" Licensing Boards Exemption for Social Work Licensure
Kansas	KAN. ADMIN. REGS. § 91–1–203 (2005)	§ 91–1–203 Licensure requirements. (a)Conditional Licenses (3) Each applicant for a conditional school specialist license shall submit to the state board the following: (A) An official transcript verifying the granting of a graduate degree; (B) verification from an accredited institution by the unit head or designee of completion of a graduate-level school specialist program; (C) verification of at least one year of recent accredited experience or at least eight semester hours of recent credit; (D) verification of a minimum 3.25 cumulative GPA on a 4.0 scale in graduate coursework; (E) if application is made for a library media specialist endorsement, school counselor endorsement, or reading specialist endorsement, a currently valid professional teaching license; (F) verification of successful completion of a school specialist assessment as determined by the state board; (G) an application for conditional school specialist license; and (H) the licensure fee.

(b) Professional licenses … (3) Each applicant for an initial professional school specialist license shall submit to the state board the following: (A) Verification of successful completion of the school specialist performance assessment prescribed by the state board while employed in a school accredited by the state board or by a national or regional accrediting agency recognized by the state board; (B) verification of at least one year of recent accredited experience or at least eight semester hours of recent credit; (C) an application for professional school specialist license; and (D) the licensure fee. | No exemption from social work licensing requirements |

State	School Social Worker Certification Relevant Statute	Relevant Text	State(s) "Professional" Licensing Boards Exemption for Social Work Licensure
Kentucky	16 Ky. Admin. Regs. 2:070 (2003)	§ 16 KAR 2:070. Professional certificate for school social worker. **Section 1.** (1) The professional certificate for school social worker shall be issued to an applicant who has: (a) Completed a Master's of Social Work (MSW) degree: 1. With: a. A cumulative minimum grade point average of 2.50 on a 4.00 scale; or b. A minimum grade point average of 3.00 on a 4.00 scale on the last sixty (60) hours of credit completed, including undergraduate and graduate coursework; and 2. Accredited by the Council on Social Work Education; and (b) Completed an approved program of preparation for school social worker. (2) The initial professional certificate for school social worker shall be issued for u validity period of five (5) years. (3) The professional certificate for school social worker shall be renewed based upon the renewal requirements established in 16 KAR 4:060. (4) To apply for the professional certificate for school social worker, the applicant shall submit a completed Form TC-1 to the Education Professional Standards Board. (5) The professional certificate for school social worker shall be valid for providing school social work services for all grade levels in the public schools or an accredited nonpublic school. **Section 2.** (1) The approved program of preparation shall be based upon the Standards for School Social Work Services established by the National Association of Social Workers. (2) (a) The program of preparation shall be submitted to the Education Professional Standards Board for approval pursuant to the requirements established in 16 KAR 5:010. (b) The program of preparation shall be submitted through the institutional unit for educator preparation. **Section 3.** Incorporation by Reference. (1) The following material is incorporated by reference: (a) Form TC-1, rev. 10/02, Education Professional Standards Board; and (b) National Association of Social Workers Standards for School Social Work Services, June 18, 1992. (2) This material may be inspected, copied, or obtained, subject to applicable copyright law, at the Education Professional Standards Board, 100 Airport Road, 3rd Floor, Frankfort, Kentucky 40601, Monday through Friday, 8 a.m. to 4:30 p.m. (See also § 16 KAR 2:080. Provisional and probationary certificates for school social worker.)	See Ky. Rev. Stat. Ann. § 335.010 (1996) Employees of the State Department of Education or local boards of education Employees of the Commonwealth of Kentucky, the director or administrative head of a social service agency or division of a city, county or urban-county government, or applicants for such employment to be licensed

State	School Social Worker Certification Relevant Statute	Relevant Text	State(s) "Professional" Licensing Boards Exemption for Social Work Licensure
Louisiana	LA ADMIN. CODE tit. 28, § 413 (2006)	§ 413. Social Worker. A. Social Worker—issued to individuals with master's degrees in social work or social welfare. B. Provisional School Social Worker—valid for three years. 1. Eligibility requirements: a. a provisional Graduate Social Work Certificate (GSW) issued under R.S. 37:2701 et seq; b. an individual must work under the supervision of a Licensed Clinical Social Worker (LCSW) for a minimum of one hour per week if providing clinical social work services. 2. Renewal guidelines: nonrenewable. C. Qualified School Social Worker 1. Eligibility requirements-one of the following: a. Licensed Clinical Social Worker (LCSW), in accordance with R.S.37:2701 et seq. b. Certificate as a Graduate Social Worker (GSW), in accordance with R.S. 37:201et seq.; receive a minimum of one hour per week of supervision by a LCSW, if providing clinical social work services; and have work experience in one or more of the following social work practice settings within the past five years: i. school setting; ii. mental health setting; iii. correction setting; iv. family/child/community service agency; v. medical social services in which social services were delivered to families and children; vi. private clinical practice in which social work services were delivered to adults, children, and families; or vii. have graduate Social Worker field experience in the above Social Work practice settings plus two years of work experience, to be judged by the Louisiana State Board of Certified Social Work Examiners. 2. This certificate is valid provided the holder maintains current Louisiana licensure as a Social Worker. A social worker who changes employing school systems must provide a copy of his/her current Louisiana license to serve as a social worker.	No exemption from social work licensing requirements
Maine	ME. REV. STAT. ANN. tit 20-A, § 4008 (1989)	§ 4008. Privileged communications 1. Definitions. As used in this section, unless the context indicates otherwise, the following terms have the following meanings ... C. "School social worker" means a person who is employed as a school social worker in a school setting and who: (1) Is licensed as a social worker by the State Board of Social Worker Licensure; or (2) Possesses a bachelor's degree and has been granted a conditional license from the State Board of Social Worker Licensure.	No exemption from social work licensing requirements
Maryland	MD. CODE REGS. 13A.12.03.11 (2005)	§ 13A.12.03.11 School Social Worker. A. To obtain certification as a school social worker, the applicant shall be licensed by the Maryland State Board of Social Work Examiners as a: (1) Graduate social worker; (2) Certified social worker; or (3) Certified social worker-clinical. B. On or after December 1, 2008, but not later than March 31, 2009, the Maryland State Board of Education shall initiate a review to consider amending this regulation to include additional criteria to obtain certification as a school social worker, if such criteria are considered appropriate.	No exemption from social work licensing requirements

State	School Social Worker Certification Relevant Statute	Relevant Text	State(s) "Professional" Licensing Boards Exemption for Social Work Licensure
Massachusetts	603 MASS. CODE REGS. 7.11 (2004)	§ 7.11: Professional Support Personnel Licenses. Candidates seeking professional support personnel licenses who have substantial experience and formal education relevant to the license sought but who do not meet all of the specific requirements listed in 603 CMR 7.11 may demonstrate that they meet the requirements, with the exception of a passing score on the Communication and Literacy Skills test, through a Panel Review administered by the Department in accordance with guidelines to be established by the Department. For candidates who were prepared outside Massachusetts, *see* 603 CMR 7.04(2)(d) and 7.05(5)(a) and (b). (4) School Social Worker/School Adjustment Counselor (Levels: All)	*See* MASS. GEN. LAWS ch. 112 § 134 (1977) Social work students Individuals employed in state, county, or municipal governmental agencies
		(a) Initial License. 1. Master's degree in Social Work or Counseling. 2. Course work and clinical experience that demonstrate knowledge of: a. Principles of therapeutic relationships. b. Theories of normal and abnormal intellectual, social, and emotional development. c. Learning disorders, including emotional issues affecting student achievement, and their treatment. d. Prevention and treatment of substance abuse, physical and sexual abuse, and violence in PreK-12 students. e. Knowledge of state-of-the-art diagnostic instruments; procedures for testing and interpreting results. f. Techniques for communicating and working with families and school and community personnel. g. Knowledge of the criminal justice system with particular reference to the juvenile justice system and organizations. h. Knowledge of medical conditions and medication related to physical disabilities and learning disorders. i. Federal and state laws and regulations addressing the legal rights of students and families. 3. A practicum of 900 hours, 450 of which must be working with children, adolescents, and families in an educational setting. 4. Passing score on the Communication and Literacy Skills test.	
		(b) Professional License. 1. Possession of an Initial license as a school social worker/school adjustment counselor. 2. Three years of employment as a school social worker or school adjustment counselor. 3. Completion of one of the following: a. A total of 60 credits of graduate coursework that may include credits earned in a master's degree program for the Initial license in a discipline appropriate to the license sought including but not limited to mental health counseling, psychological counseling, school counseling, school social work, or social work. b. Achievement and maintenance of a certificate or license from one of the following: i. The Massachusetts Board of Registration of Social Work, as a Licensed Certified Social Worker (LCSW) or a Licensed Independent Clinical Social Worker (LICSW). ii. The Massachusetts Board of Allied Mental Health Professionals, as a Licensed Mental Health Counselor (LMHC), a Licensed Marriage and Family Therapist (LMFT), or a Licensed Rehabilitation Counselor (LRC).	

State	School Social Worker Certification Relevant Statute	Relevant Text	State(s) "Professional" Licensing Boards Exemption for Social Work Licensure
Michigan	MICH. ADMIN. CODE r. 340.1012 (1979)	R 340.1012 Qualifications of school social worker. Rule 2. (1) For approval as a school social worker, an applicant shall have completed a master's degree from a graduate school of social work program approved by the state board of education. The degree program shall consist of a 2-year graduate course or equivalent, including appropriate methods courses and a minimum of a 500 clock hour supervised social work practicum. (2) In addition to the requirements of subrule (1), an applicant for temporary approval as a school social worker shall have submitted to the department of education a written recommendation for temporary approval from the approved university school of social work training program. Temporary approval shall be granted a school social worker for the initial year of service. (3) Full approval as a school social worker shall be contingent upon written documentation from the employing school district of satisfactory completion of 1 year as a school social worker with direction from a fully approved school social worker, or as otherwise authorized by the state board of education. (4) A previously approved school social worker who has not been employed as a school social worker in an approved program in Michigan for 5 or more consecutive years shall obtain re-approval from the state board of education as a condition of reemployment.	No exemption from social work licensing requirements
Minnesota	MINN. R. 8710–6300 (2001)	8710.6300 SCHOOL SOCIAL WORKER. Subp. 2. Requirements for first professional license. A candidate for licensure as a school social worker shall: A. hold a baccalaureate or master's degree in social work from a program accredited by the Council on Social Work Education; and B. be currently licensed in Minnesota to practice as a social worker under the Board of Social Work.	*See* MINN. STAT. § 148D.065 (2006) Students City, county, and state agency social workers Tribes and private nonprofit agencies; voluntary licensure
Mississippi	No specific provision with regards to certification requirements for School Social Workers.		No exemption from social work licensing requirements
Missouri	No specific provision with regards to certification requirements for School Social Workers.		No exemption from social work licensing requirements
Montana	No specific provision with regards to certification requirements for School Social Workers.		*See* MONT. CODE ANN. § 37–22–305 (2005) If the Social Worker is an exclusive employee of a municipal, state, or federal agency then they are exempt from the licensing requirements of the Board of Social Work Examiners and Professional Counselors.
Nebraska	No specific provision with regards to certification requirements for School Social Workers.		No exemption from social work licensing requirements

State	School Social Worker Certification Relevant Statute	Relevant Text	State(s) "Professional" Licensing Boards Exemption for Social Work Licensure
Nevada	Nev. Admin. Code § 391.320 (1991)	NAC 391.320 Endorsement to serve as social worker. (NRS 391.019) 1. To receive an endorsement to serve as a social worker, a person must: (a) Hold a current license issued by the Board of Examiners for Social Workers; and (b) Have completed an educational program for social workers in schools which includes a practicum in schools. 2. In addition to the requirements listed in subsection 1, a person who wishes to receive such an endorsement must: (a) Have completed a program to serve as a social worker in schools that is approved by the Board; (b) Hold the credential issued by the National Association of Social Workers certifying that the holder is a specialist in social work in schools; or (c) Hold a master's degree in social work from a college or university that has been accredited by the Council on Social Work Education. 3. To renew the endorsement, the holder must: (a) Have completed at least 6 semester hours in education relating to social work in schools or an equal amount of credit for in-service work relating to social work in schools; and (b) Continue to hold a valid license issued by the Board of Examiners for Social Workers.	Not Applicable
New Hampshire	N.H. Code Admin. R. Ann. Ed 507.14 (2004)	Ed 507.14 Social Worker. For an individual to be certified as a social worker, the individual shall hold a bachelor's degree in social work from a college or university approved by the New Hampshire post secondary education commission.	See N.H. Rev. Stat. Ann. § 330-A:34 (2005) In the employ of a federal, state, county, or municipal agency Student/intern
New Jersey	N.J. Admin. Code § 6A:9–13.5 (2006)	6A:9–13.5 School social worker. (a) The school social worker endorsement authorizes the holder to serve as a school social worker in any school district in the State in grades preschool through 12. (b) To be eligible for the standard educational services certificate with a school social worker endorsement, the candidate shall hold a master's degree from a regionally accredited college or university and complete a total of 30 graduate-level semester hour credits with a study in each of the areas listed below: 1. Psychology, including general psychology, educational psychology, psychology of adolescence and child growth and development; 2. Special education and/or learning disabilities; 3. Social problems, including study in dealing with delinquency, poverty, interracial and intercultural problems; 4. A minimum of six semester-hour credits in social case work, introductory and advanced, including principles and practices in social case work, interviewing, and methods and skills in diagnosis; 5. Mental hygiene and social psychiatry, including dynamics of human behavior and psychopathology; 6. Medical information, including the role of the social worker in health problems or fundamentals of substance abuse and dependency; 7. Community organizations, agencies and resources; and 8. Social policy and public welfare services, including the care and protection of at-risk children and families. (c) Holders of a master's degree in social work from a regionally accredited college or university will be issued a standard educational services certificate with a school social worker endorsement.	See N.J. Admin. Code § 45:15BB-5.c (1991) Student/intern School social workers Alcohol/drug abuse intervention State employees

State	School Social Worker Certification Relevant Statute	Relevant Text	State(s) "Professional" Licensing Boards Exemption for Social Work Licensure
New Mexico	N.M. Code R. § 6.63.7.4 (1993)	6.63.7.8 REQUIREMENTS: Persons seeking licensure in school social work, grades pre k-12 pursuant to the provisions of this rule shall meet the following requirements of Subsections A or B or C of 6.63.7.8 NMAC; A. Level 1, entry level school social worker (1) Bachelor's or master's degree in social work from a regionally accredited college or university and meeting the applicable program requirements as follows: (a) the bachelor's or master's degree awarded by a New Mexico college or university must incorporate the New Mexico public education department's (PED) approved competencies in the area of social work; OR (b) the bachelor's or master's degree awarded by a college or university outside of New Mexico must be for a social work program approved by the PED; AND (2) valid social work license issued by the New Mexico social work examiners board. B. Level 2, school social worker (1) valid level 1 school social work license; (2) verification by the superintendent of the local school district or the governing authority of the private school or state institution that the social worker has satisfactorily demonstrated the entry level social work competencies approved by the PED; AND (3) valid social work license issued by the New Mexico social work examiners board. C. Level 3, independent school social worker (1) master's degree in social work from a regionally accredited college or university; (2) valid level 2 school social work license; (3) valid independent social worker license issued by the New Mexico board of social work examiners with specializations in clinical social work or school social work; (4) evidence of a minimum of 875 hours of supervised experience in providing therapeutic services to children, including children with severe emotional disturbances and behavioral disorders, in the school setting; AND (5) verification by the superintendent of the local school district or the governing authority of the private school or state institution that the social worker has satisfactorily demonstrated the independent social worker competencies approved by the PED.	No exemption from social work licensing requirements

State	School Social Worker Certification Relevant Statute	Relevant Text	State(s) "Professional" Licensing Boards Exemption for Social Work Licensure
New York	N.Y. Comp. Codes R. & Regs. Tit. 8 § 80–2.3 (2005)	Section 80–2.3 Certificates valid for pupil personnel service (school attendance teacher, school counselor, school dental hygiene teacher, school nurse-teacher, school psychologist and school social worker). Preparation: to obtain a certificate in a pupil personnel service, a candidate shall meet the requirements set forth in this section ... (f) *School social worker.* (1) Provisional certificate. (i) The candidate shall hold a baccalaureate degree from a regionally accredited institution of higher education or from an institution approved by the department, and in addition shall have completed 30 semester hours of graduate study, including a supervised internship, in the field of social work. (ii) Time validity. The provisional certificate shall be valid for five years from date of issuance. (2) Permanent certificate. The candidate shall have completed two years of school experience in the field of pupil personnel services, hold the degree of master of social work or an equivalent degree as determined by the department, and be licensed and registered by the department as a licensed master social worker or a licensed clinical social worker.	No exemption from social work licensing requirements
North Carolina	16 N.C. Admin. Code 6C.0304 (2003)	16 NC ADC 6C.0304 LICENSE PATTERNS (a) Licenses shall indicate grade levels, content areas and specializations for which the professional shall be eligible for employment. (b) Licenses shall be of the following types: ... (3) Student services area. The holder may provide specialized assistance to the learner, the teacher, the administrator, and the education program in general. This category shall include school counseling, school social work ... There shall be three levels of preparation as in the case of the administrator/supervisor, except that school psychology shall be restricted to the sixth-year or doctorate levels and school social work may be earned at the bachelor's level. (c) The department shall base license classification on the level and degree of career development and competence. There shall be two classifications of licenses: (1) The Standard Professional License I, which shall be valid for three years, shall allow the holder to begin practicing the profession on an independent basis in North Carolina. To be issued a Standard Professional License I, the individual must complete a teacher education program approved in accordance with these Rules and meet the federal requirement to be designated "highly qualified." (2) The Standard Professional License II shall authorize professional school service on an ongoing basis, subject to renewal every five years.	No exemption from social work licensing requirements
North Dakota	No specific provision with regards to certification requirements for School Social Workers.		No exemption from social work licensing requirements

State	School Social Worker Certification Relevant Statute	Relevant Text	State(s) "Professional" Licensing Boards Exemption for Social Work Licensure
Ohio	Ohio Admin. Code 3301: 24–05 (2004)	3301–24–05 Licensure. (d) School social worker (i) Master's degree in social work, and(ii) The requirements specified in paragraph (F)(1) of this rule; and (iii) One year of successful experience in a chartered school or school district under a professional license; or one year of social work experience under a current license issued by the Ohio counselor and social worker board; or a graduate level social work practicum of at least ten weeks in a chartered school or school district; and (iv) Current license to practice social work issued by the Ohio counselor and social worker board …	Ohio Rev. Code Ann. § 4757.41 (2002) Educators Civil service employees Students
Oklahoma	No specific provision with regards to certification requirements for School Social Workers.		No exemption from social work licensing requirements
Oregon	Or. Admin. R. 584–070–0310 (1999)	§ 584–070–0310 Limited Student Service License (1) To be eligible for a Limited Student Service License the applicant must have a bachelor's degree or higher from a regionally accredited institution in the United States, or the foreign equivalent of such degree approved by the commission, together with an equally valid master's degree or other specialized preparation related to the intended service role and ordinarily equivalent to one academic year of graduate study. The applicant also must demonstrate knowledge of applicable civil rights laws and furnish fingerprints in the manner prescribed by the commission. An applicant without an approved first aid card must obtain one within 90 days of receiving the license … (3) The holder of a Limited Student Service License shall use only the title specifically approved by the commission and shall not use any unapproved title or imply any unapproved function. Titles such as "advisor" or "student service specialist" will more readily be approved. The following provisos apply … (b) The commission at its discretion may consider a title indicating a therapeutic student service role like counseling or social work, for a specialist who has a corresponding master's or doctor's degree, if the applicant is licensed by the Board of Licensed Professional Counselors and Therapists or is demonstrably prevented from gaining admission to a graduate program in school counseling or school psychology and therefore cannot reasonably be required to apply for a non-renewable transitional license. (c) The commission will ordinarily approve an appropriate social work title for an applicant licensed by the Board of Clinical Social Workers. (4) To be eligible for renewal of the Limited Student Service License, an applicant must obtain a passing score as currently specified by the commission on a test of basic verbal and computational skills, unless the applicant held an Oregon educator license before 1985 or has a regionally accredited doctor's degree. The applicant must also obtain a passing score on a test of knowledge of U.S. and Oregon civil rights laws at the conclusion of a course or workshop approved by the commission.	No exemption from social work licensing requirements

State	School Social Worker Certification Relevant Statute	Relevant Text	State(s) "Professional" Licensing Boards Exemption for Social Work Licensure
Pennsylvania	22 Pa. Code § 49.102 (2006)	§ 49.102. Educational Specialist I. (a) The Educational Specialist I Certificate is valid for 6 years of service in public schools in this Commonwealth in each area for which it is endorsed. It may be converted to an Educational Specialist II Certificate in any endorsement area as provided in § 49.103 (relating to Educational Specialist II). (b) The Educational Specialist I Certificate will be issued to applicants who: (1) Present evidence of successful completion of a Department-approved educational specialist preparation program or its equivalent. (2) Present evidence of satisfactory achievement in assessments prescribed by the Department under § 49.18(a) (relating to assessment). (3) Receive recommendation for certification from a college or university if completing a Department-approved educational specialist preparation program. (See also § 49.103. Educational Specialist II.)	No exemption from social work licensing requirements
Rhode Island	08–010–012 R.I. Code R. § 20 (1999)	§ 08 010 012. Individual Professional Development Plan (I-Plan) Certification and Endorsements. Section 20. School Social Worker. The School Social Worker certificate is valid for service as a School Social Worker in grades PK — 12. I. Certificate of Eligibility for Employment (CEE) — Valid for Three (3) Years. The initial certificate in Rhode Island for all areas of certification is a CEE. The CEE is used to seek regular employment in the schools of Rhode Island for the field identified on the CEE. The CEE is also valid for service as a substitute teacher. If regular employment is not secured in the three (3) year period, the CEE can be renewed every three (3) years (SEE NOTE ONE) until regular employment is secured. To be issued a CEE as a school social worker an individual needs to satisfy all of the following: Bachelor's degree from an accredited or an approved institution of higher education as defined in these regulations. A Master's Degree in Social Work from a school accredited by the Council on Social Work Education. Licensed as a certified Social Worker by the Rhode Island State Board of Registration for Social Workers. II. Professional Certificate — Valid for Five (5) Years The professional certificate is issued to individuals who secure regular employment in the schools of Rhode Island. Upon securing regular employment in Rhode Island, the CEE is used to request a five (5) year professional certificate. When applying for a five (5) year professional certificate the applicant must submit the CEE along with documentation from the employing authority that regular employment has been secured in the certification area of the CEE. Upon securing regular employment, the educator must write and get approved a five (5) year Individual Professional Development Plan (I-Plan). The professional certificate may be renewed every five (5) years upon the successful completion of an (I-Plan) that has been approved by the I-Plan Review Panel. Individuals who have not served as a school social worker in Rhode Island for the five (5) year period are entitled to an extension to the professional certificate (SEE NOTE TWO) at the end of each five (5) year period without the completion of an I-Plan.	No exemption from social work licensing requirements

State	School Social Worker Certification Relevant Statute	Relevant Text	State(s) "Professional" Licensing Boards Exemption for Social Work Licensure
South Carolina	S.C. CODE ANN. REGS. 43–51 (2003)	§ 43–51 Certification Requirements. I. Requirements for Certification The applicant must meet all requirements for certification that are in effect in the current application year (July 1-June 30). The responsibility for providing accurate and complete documentation of eligibility for certification is that of the applicant. To qualify for certification in South Carolina, the applicant must fulfill the following requirements: A. Earn a bachelor's or master's degree either from an institution that has a state-approved teacher education program and is accredited for general collegiate purposes by a regional accreditation association, or from a South Carolina institution that has programs approved for teacher education by the State Board of Education, or from an institution that has programs approved for teacher education by the National Council for Accreditation of Teacher Education (NCATE). Professional education credit must be earned through an institution that has a teacher education program approved for initial certification. 1. Graduate degrees acceptable for certificate advancement include academic or professional degrees in the field of education or in an academic area for which a corresponding or relevant teaching area is authorized by the State Board of Education. 2. All credit at the graduate level must be earned through the graduate school of an institution that is accredited for general collegiate purposes by a regional accreditation association and that has a regular graduate division that meets regional accreditation requirements. Graduate credit can also be earned through a South Carolina institution that has graduate programs approved for teacher education by the State Board of Education or through an institution that has graduate programs approved for teacher education by the National Council for Accreditation of Teacher Education (NCATE). B. Submit the required teacher area examination score(s) as adopted by the State Board of Education for purposes of certification. Effective July 1, 2006, the required score on the examination of general professional knowledge (pedagogy) as adopted by the State Board of Education for purposes of certification will be required for initial certification. Until that date, the general professional knowledge (pedagogy) examination will be required only for professional certification. C. Be at least eighteen years of age. D. Undergo a criminal records check by the South Carolina Law Enforcement Division and a national criminal records check supported by fingerprints conducted by the Federal Bureau of Investigation. If the applicant does not complete the initial certification process within eighteen months from the original date of application, the FBI fingerprint process must be repeated. Eligible applicants who have prior arrests and/or convictions must undergo a review by the State Board of Education and be approved before a certificate can be issued to them. Background checks from other states are not transferable to South Carolina.	No exemption from social work licensing requirements

State	School Social Worker Certification Relevant Statute	Relevant Text	State(s) "Professional" Licensing Boards Exemption for Social Work Licensure
South Dakota	S.D. Admin. R. 24:16:10:06 (2006)	§ 24:16:10:06. (Effective through June 30, 2008) Preschool to grade 12 school social work education program. A preschool to grade 12 school social work education program shall require a master's degree in social work, which includes the following: (1) A concentration of coursework social work in nature, including social work foundations assessment, and interventions; (2) The study of human behavior in the social environment; social work with individuals, groups, and communities; (3) A supervised internship in a social work agency for a period of one semester; and (4) A study and/or experience in the following: (a) Demonstrated competence in social work assessment and intervention based on family systems model; (b) Knowledge of the referral process to community, public, private, medical, social, and educational agencies; (c) Advocacy for children and their families; (d) Understanding the needs of special and diverse population groups and application of the understanding in social work intervention; (e) Verification of coursework related to the operation of K-12 schools, the role of school personnel, and the role of a social worker in the school setting; or (f) Verification of a minimum of one semester of supervised internship or one year of employment in the school setting. Certification will be granted upon proper documentation, by the Department of Education as a School Service Specialist and with documentation of a license by the South Dakota Board of Social Work Examiners.	No exemption from social work licensing requirements
Tennessee	Tenn. Comp. R. & Regs. 0520–2–3.01	§ 0520–2–3–.01. LICENSURE, GENERAL REQUIREMENTS. (15) Candidates seeking licensure and endorsement as a school social worker shall complete a program in social work either at the bachelor's or master's level; candidates shall also complete a program of studies in school social work approved by the State Board of Education. Candidates must be recommended by an institution of higher education with a preparation program approved according to standards and guidelines established by the State Board of Education.	No exemption from social work licensing requirements
Texas	Tex. Educ. Code Ann. § 21.003 (1995)	§ 21.003. Certification Required. (b) A person may not be employed by a school district as an audiologist, occupational therapist, physical therapist, physician, nurse, school psychologist, associate school psychologist, social worker, or speech language pathologist unless the person is licensed by the state agency that licenses that profession. A person may perform specific services within those professions for a school district only if the person holds the appropriate credential from the appropriate state agency.	No exemption from social work licensing requirements

State	School Social Worker Certification Relevant Statute	Relevant Text	State(s) "Professional" Licensing Boards Exemption for Social Work Licensure
Utah	UTAH ADMIN. CODE r. 277–505–4 (2002)	§ R277–506–4. School Social Workers. A. An applicant for the Level 1 School Social Worker License area of concentration shall have: (1) completed a Board approved program for the preparation of school social workers including a Master of Social Work degree from an accredited institution; (2) demonstrated competence in the following: (a) articulating the role and function of the school social worker including relationships with other professional school and community personnel, organizations, and agencies; (b) understanding the organization, administration, and evaluation of a school social work program; (c) social work practice with individuals, families, and groups; (d) developing and interpreting a social history and psycho-social assessment of the individual and the family system; (e) analyzing family dynamics and experience in counseling and conflict management and resolution; (f) communication and consulting skills in working with the client, the family, the school staff, and community and social agencies; (g) understanding the teaching/learning environment; (h) analyzing school law and child welfare issues; (i) using social work methods to facilitate the affective domain of education and the learning process; and (j) understanding knowledge pertaining to the cause and effects of social forces, cultural changes, stress, disability, disease, deprivation, neglect, and abuse on learning and on human behavior and development, and the effect of these forces on minorities of race, ethnicity, and class. (3) completed an approved school social work internship in a school setting or in an agency which includes a substantial amount of experience with children and contact with schools; and (4) been recommended by an institution whose program of preparation for social workers has been approved by the Board. B. An applicant for the Level 2-Standard School Social Worker License area of concentration shall have: (1) completed at least three years of successful experience as a school social worker under a Level 1 School Social Worker License area of concentration or its equivalent; and (2) been recommended by the employing school district with consultation from a teacher education institution. C. The social worker program of an institution may be approved by the Board if it meets the standards prescribed in the Standards for State Approval of Teacher Education for school social workers, developed and available as provided in R277–506–3D.	No exemption from social work licensing requirements

State	School Social Worker Certification Relevant Statute	Relevant Text	State(s) "Professional" Licensing Boards Exemption for Social Work Licensure
Vermont	22–000–010 Vt. Code R. § 5440–54 (2003)	22 000 010. Licensing Regulations (5000). § 5440–54 The holder is authorized to provide school social work services to students and their families in grades PK—12. In order to qualify for this endorsement, the candidate shall demonstrate the following: . . . Additional Requirements: A master's degree, or the equivalent, in social work. A supervised internship experience (600 clock hours) in social work with a minimum of 60 hours of experience in school social work at both the elementary (PK-6) and middle/secondary (7–12) levels, under the supervision of a licensed school social worker.	No exemption from social work licensing requirements
Virginia	Va. Admin. Code § 20–21–630 (1998)	8 VAC 20–21–630. School social worker. B. Endorsement requirements. 1. Option I. The candidate must have: a. An earned master's of social work from an accredited school of social work with a minimum of 60 graduate semester hours; b. A minimum of six graduate semester hours in education; and c. Completed a supervised practicum or field experience of a minimum of 400 clock hours in an accredited school discharging the duties of a school social worker. 2. Option II. The candidate must have: a. An earned master's of social work from an accredited school of social work with a minimum of 60 graduate semester hours; b. A minimum of six graduate semester hours in education; and c. One year of successful full-time supervised experience as a school social worker in an accredited school.	See Va. Code Ann. § 54.1–3701 (1988) Social work student Federal, state, and local government employees

State	School Social Worker Certification Relevant Statute	Relevant Text	State(s) "Professional" Licensing Boards Exemption for Social Work Licensure
Washington	WASH. ADMIN CODE 181–79A-221 (1999)	§ 181–79A-221. Academic and experience requirements for certification—School counselors, school psychologists, and school social workers. (3) School social worker. (a) Initial. (i) The candidate shall have completed all requirements for a master's degree in social work except special projects or thesis. (ii) The candidate shall have successfully completed a written comprehensive examination of the knowledge included in the course work for the required master's degree. This examination shall be an examination from a regionally accredited institution of higher education, the social worker examination of the Academy of Certified Social Workers or the National Teacher Examination—School Social Worker Specialty Area examination required for certification as a school social worker by the National Association of Social Workers. (b) Residency. (i) The candidate shall hold a master's degree in social work. (ii) The candidate shall have successfully completed a written comprehensive examination of the knowledge included in the course work for the required master's degree. This examination shall be a proctored, written examination of a regionally accredited institution of higher education or the candidate may meet the requirement by receiving a passing score on the Praxis II school social work examination administered by Educational Testing Service (ETS). (c) Continuing. (i) The candidate shall hold a master's degree in social work. (ii) The candidate shall provide documentation of one hundred eighty days or full-time equivalent or more employment in the respective role with an authorized employer—i.e., school district, educational service district, state agency, college or university, private school, or private school system—and at least thirty days of such employment with the same employer. (iii) The candidates must demonstrate their respective knowledge and skills while employed in that role by passing a one-quarter or one-semester college or university course that includes peer review. The college or university shall establish the procedures for the peer review with advice from the respective professional education advisory board. (d) Professional. The candidate shall have completed an approved professional certificate program.	No exemption from social work licensing requirements
West Virginia	W. VA. CODE R. § 18–1–1 (2003)	§ 18–1–1. Definitions ... (i) "Social worker" means a non-teaching school employee who, at a minimum, possesses an undergraduate degree in social work from an accredited institution of higher learning and who provides various professional social work services, activities or methods as defined by the state board for the benefit of students ...	W. VA. CODE § 30–30–6 (1984) Employed by school board Social work student

State	School Social Worker Certification Relevant Statute	Relevant Text	State(s) "Professional" Licensing Boards Exemption for Social Work Licensure
Wisconsin	WIS. ADMIN. CODE PI § 34.31 (2000)	PI 34.31 Pupil services categories ... (4) SCHOOL SOCIAL WORKER. (a) A license may be issued to an applicant who has obtained an institutional endorsement and has completed or possesses all of the following: 1. A master's degree in social work. 2. Completion of one of the following: a. Two years successful experience as a school social worker under the supervision of a cooperating school social worker and a written recommendation from the school system administration. b. An internship in school social work under the supervision of a cooperating school social worker and a written recommendation from the school system administration. The internship shall be part of the approved program. (b) If the requirements under par. (a) 2. are not met, a 3-year nonrenewable license may be issued to an applicant who has completed all of the following: 1. At least 2 years of social work experience dealing with children and youth. One year of this experience shall be completed at the elementary, middle, or secondary level in a school, or in an agency whose major responsibility is to serve children and youth and whose program is recognized by the institution. 2. Institutional endorsement.	WIS. STAT. 457.02 (1988) School social worker

State	School Social Worker Certification Relevant Statute	Relevant Text	State(s) "Professional" Licensing Boards Exemption for Social Work Licensure
Wyoming	Westlaw Citation — WY ADC COM TSD Ch. 11 §4	Section 4. School Social Worker Program Approval Standards. The following Standards pertain to advanced programs which prepare a school social worker. (a) Standard I. The program shall require knowledge of the role and function of the school social worker and the school social work program, including relationships with other professional school personnel and community agencies and organizations. (b) Standard II. The program shall require demonstrated competence in: (i) assessment in social, emotional, behavioral and adaptive areas; (ii) individual counseling; (iii) group counseling; (iv) family dynamics and interaction; (v) crisis intervention; (vi) consultation; (vii) communication skill; (viii) referral process and utilization of resources; (ix) legal issues pertaining to the welfare of children; (x) conflict management/resolution. (c) Standard III. The program shall require knowledge of the school as an organization with emphasis on school curriculum and school law. (d) Standard IV. The program shall require knowledge of human growth and development particularly as it relates to the dynamics of the learner and the learning process. (e) Standard V. The program shall require demonstrated competence in the use of social work methods to facilitate the affective domain of education. (f) Standard VI. The program shall require knowledge of the cause and effect of life stresses such as educational handicaps, family disruption, health issues, abuse and neglect, race, ethnicity, socioeconomic and environmental factors on learning, behavior, and development. (g) Standard VII. The program shall require demonstrated competence in conducting and interpreting research with regard to community, family, and student problems relevant to services provided by the school social worker. (h) Standard VIII. The program shall require a supervised practicum in a recognized k-12 school setting.	WYO. STAT. ANN. § 33–38–103 (2001) Student school social workers

Appendix B

Supplemental Materials

The following is a list of resources published by NASW Press, which may be of interest to school social workers. Brief synopses of these publications and ordering information can be found at **http://www.naswpress.org**.

NASW Press, 2008–2009

- Frederick G. Reamer and Deborah H. Siegel, *Finding Help for Struggling Teens: A Guide for Parents and the Professionals Who Work with Them* (2006).

- Joan Pennell and Gary R. Anderson, *Widening the Circle: The Practice and Evaluation of Family Group Conference with children, Youths, and their Families* (2006).

- Lawrence B. Rosenfeld, et al., *When Their World Falls Apart: Helping Families and Children Manage the Effects of Disaster* (2005).

- *Risk and Resilience in Childhood: An Ecological Perspective* (Mark W. Fraser eds., 2nd ed. 2004)

- Mark W. Fraser, et al., *Making Choices: Social Problem-solving Skills for Children* (2000).

- Mark A. Mattaini, *Peace Power for Adolescents: Strategies for a Culture of Nonviolence* (2001).

- *Youth Violence: Current Research and Recent Practice Innovations* (Jeffrey M. Jenson and Matthew O. Howard eds., 1999).

- *School Social Work Worldwide* (Marion Huxtable and Eric Blyth eds., 2002).

- *NASW Standards for the Practice of Social Work with Adolescents*, http://www.socialworkers.org/practice/standards/NASWAdolescentsStandards.pdf (NASW ed., 2003).

- *NASW Standards for Social Work Practice In Child Welfare*, http://www.socialworkers.org/practice/standards/NASWChildWelfareStandards0905.pdf (NASW ed., 2005).

- *NASW STANDARDS FOR SCHOOL SOCIAL WORK SERVICES*, http://www.socialworkers.org/practice/standards/NASW_SSWS.pdf (NASW ed., 2002).
- Brochure: *School Social Workers: Enhancing School Success for All Students* (NASW)
- Brochure: *Gangs and Youth* (NASW)
- Brochure: *Youth Bullying: How Social Workers Can Help* (NASW)
- Periodical: *Children and Schools* (NASW)

NASW Press, 2007

MULTISYSTEM SKILLS AND INTERVENTIONS IN SCHOOL SOCIAL WORK PRACTICE (Edith M. Freeman, et al., 1998).

Endnotes

1. National Association of Social Workers, *Education of Children and Youths, in* Social Work Speaks: National Association of Social Workers Policy Statements 111, 114 (7th ed. 2003).

2. *Plyler v. Doe, 457* U.S. 202, 221 (1981) (citing *San Antonio Indep. Sch. Dist. v. Rodriguez,* 411 U.S. 1, 35 (1973)).

3. *Id.* at 223.

4. NASW, *Education of Children and Youths, supra* note 1, at 114.

5. *Id.*

6. Edith M. Freeman, *School Social Work Overview, in* Encyclopedia of Social Work 2087, 2087 (Richard L. Edwards et al. eds., 19th ed. 1995).

7. *Id.*

8. *Id.*

9. *Id.* at 2088.

10. *Id.* at 2087.

11. *Id.*

12. NASW, *Education of Children and Youths, supra* note 1, at 114.

13. Santos Torres, Jr., *Licensing, Certification, and Credentialing of School Social Workers and Other School Mental Health Professionals, in* The School Services Sourcebook: A Guide for School-Based Professionals 1121, 1121 (Cynthia Franklin, PhD, et al. eds., 2006).

14. National Association of Social Workers, *NASW Standards for School Social Work Services* 5 (2002), *available at* http://www.socialworkers.org/practice/standards/NASW_SSWS.pdf (last visited on March 4, 2008).

15. *Id.* at 6.

16. *Id.*

17. *Id.*

18. National Association of Social Workers, *Certified School Social Work Specialist: Information Booklet with Application and Reference Forms* 1, 5 (revised 2006), *available at* http://www.socialworkers.org/credentials/specialty/applications/c-ssws.pdf (last visited on April 21, 2008).

19. *Id.* at 2.

20. *Id.*

21. 16 Ky. Admin. Regs. 2:070 (2003); Wash. Admin. Code 181–79A-221 (1999).

22. Arkansas, Colorado, Connecticut, Delaware, District of Columbia, Idaho, Illinois, Indiana, Iowa, Kansas, Kentucky, Louisiana, Massachusetts, Michigan, Nevada, New Jersey, Ohio, Rhode Island, South Dakota, Utah, Vermont, Virginia, Washington, and Wisconsin. *See* Appendix A.

23. Idaho Admin. Code r. 08.02.02.027 (2004).

24. Alaska, Florida, Georgia, Maine, Maryland, Minnesota, New Hampshire, New Mexico, New York, Oregon, South Carolina, Tennessee, and West Virginia. *See* Appendix A.

25. Ga. Comp. R. & Regs. 505–2–0.205 (2006); Me. Rev. State. Ann. tit 20-A, § 4008 (1989); N.Y. Comp. Codes R. & Regs. tit 8 § 80–2.3 (2005).

26. *See* Appendix A.

27. Alaska Admin Code tit. 4 § 12.355 (2005).

28. Conn. Agencies Regs. § 10.145D-564 (1993).

29. D.C. Mun. Regs. Tit. 5, § 1660 (1993).

30. S.D. Admin. R. 24:16:10:06 (2006).

31. Only 5 states have no exemptions (Maine, Michigan, New Mexico, Oregon, and Pennsylvania).

32. Colorado, Georgia, Indiana, Kentucky, New Jersey, Ohio, Vermont, West Virginia, Wisconsin, and Wyoming. See Appendix A.

33. *See, e.g.,* Ohio Rev. Stat. § 4757.41 ("The provisions of this act shall not apply to … ").

34. *Brown v. Bd. of Educ.,* 347 U.S. 483 (1954).

35. *Id.* at 493.

36. *Id.*

37. *Id.*

38. *Plyler v. Doe* at 230.

39. *Id.* at 221. The Court further noted that "by denying these children a basic education, we [would] deny them the ability to live within the structure of our civic institutions, and foreclose any realistic possibility that they will contribute in even the smallest way to the progress of our Nation." *Id.* at 223.

40. *Parents Involved in Comm. Schools v. Seattle School Dist. No. 1* and *Meredith v. Jefferson County Board of Educ.,* 127 S.Ct. 2738 (2007).

41. *Id.* at 2740–41.

42. It should be noted that the Supreme Court's decision that there is no compelling interest in pursuing diversity in public schools on the basis of race does not disturb the court's holding in *Grutter v. Bollinger,* 539 U.S. 306 (2003). *Id.* at 2753–54. In *Grutter,* the court found that states do have a compelling interest in promoting diversity in higher education where pursuing that interest focuses on race as only one of many factors for achieving a diverse student body. *Parents Involved in Comm. Schools,* 127 S.Ct. at 2753–54.

43. *See* Sherri Morgan and Carolyn I. Polowy, *A Review of the Supreme Court's 2007 Affirmative Action Decision,* NASW Legal Defense Fund Legal Issue of the Month, September 2007 at 2 (indicating that the opinion of Justice Kennedy is considered by many scholars to have the legal gravity of a majority opinion because it was Kennedy's swing vote that achieved the votes necessary to hand down a decision).

44. *Parents Involved in Comm. Schools,* 127 S.Ct. at 2790.

45. *Id.* at 2792.

46. *Pierce v. Society of the Sisters,* 268 U.S. 510 (1925).

47. U.S. Const. amend. I. ("Congress shall make no law … prohibiting the free exercise [of religion].")

48. *Pierce v. Society of the Sisters* at 534–535.

49. *Wisconsin v. Yoder,* 406 U.S. 205, 213–14 (1972).

50. *Id.*

51. U.S. Const. amend. I. ("Congress shall make no law … prohibiting the free exercise [of religion].")

52. *Wisconsin v. Yoder* at 211–12. Compare with *Duro v. District Attorney,* 712 F.2d 96, 98 (4th Cir. 1983) (upholding a North Carolina compulsory education law against a challenge by Pentecostal parents who wished to educate their children at home, noting that the parents, "unlike their Amish counterparts, are not members of a community which has existed for three centuries and has a long history of being a successful, self-sufficient, segment of American society").

53. *Wisconsin v. Yoder* at 235–236.

54. U.S. Const. amend. I ("Congress shall make no law respecting an establishment of religion.")

55. *Engel v. Vitale,* 370 U.S. 421 (1962).

56. *Edwards v. Aguillard*, 482 U.S. 578 (1987).

57. *Lee v. Weisman*, 505 U.S. 577 (1992).

58. *Zelman v. Simmons-Harris*, 536 U.S. 639 (2002).

59. *Id.* at 663.

60. Matthew Robb, *The ABCs of Homeschooling*, 5(5) Social Work Today 14, 17 (2005).

61. *See* Subcommittee on Human Resources of the Committee on Ways and Means, U.S. House of Representatives, 108th Congress 1st Session, November 6, 2003, *available at* http://waysandmeans. house.gov/hearings.asp?formmode=detail&hearing=113 (last visited on March 10, 2008).

62. Robb, *supra* note 60, at 17–18.

63. Ala. Code §§ 16–28–1, -3, -5; Alaska Stat. § 14.30.010(a); Ariz. Rev. Stat. Ann. § 15–802(A)(1); Ark. Code Ann. § 6–18–201; Cal. Educ. Code § 48200; Colo. Rev. Stat. Ann. § 22–33–104; Conn. Gen. Stat. Ann. § 10–184; Del. Code Ann. tit. 14, § 2702; D.C. Code Ann. § 31–202; Fla. Stat. Ann. § 1003.21; Ga. Code Ann. § 20–2–690.1; Haw. Rev. Stat. Ann. § 302A-1132; Idaho Code § 33–202; Ill. Ann. Stat. ch. 105, para. 5/26–1, Ind. Code Ann. § 20–33–2–6; Iowa Code Ann. § 299.1; Kan. Stat. Ann. § 72–1111; Ky. Rev. Stat. Ann. § 159.010; La. Rev. Stat. Ann § 17:221; Me. Rev. Stat. Ann. tit. 20-A, § 5001-A; Md. Code Ann., Educ. § 7–301(a); Mass. Gen. Laws Ann. ch. 76, § 1; Minn. Stat. Ann. § 120A.22; Miss. Code Ann. § 37–13–91; Mo. Ann. Stat. § 167.031; Mont. Code Ann. § 20–5–102; Neb. Rev. Stat. § 79–201; Nev. Rev. Stat. Ann. § 392.040; N.H. Rev. Stat. Ann. § 193:1; N.J. Stat. Ann. § 18A:38–25; N.M. Stat. Ann. § 22–12–2; N.Y. Educ. Law § 3204; N.C. Gen. Stat. § 115C-378; N.D. Cent. Code § 15.1–20–01; Ohio Rev. Code Ann. § 3321.04; Okla. Stat. Ann. tit. 70, § 10–015; Or. Rev. Stat. § 339.010; Pa. Stat. Ann. tit. 24, § 13–1327(a); R.I. Gen. Laws § 16–19–1; S.C. Code Ann. § 59–65–10; S.D. Codified Laws Ann. § 13–27–1; Tenn. Code Ann. § 49–6–3001(c); Tex. Educ. Code Ann. § 21.085; Utah Code § 53A-11–101; Vt. Stat. Ann. tit. 16, § 1121; Va. Code Ann. § 22.1–254; Wash. Rev. Code Ann. § 28A.225.010; W. Va. Code § 18–8–1; Wis. Stat. Ann. § 118.15; Wyo. Stat. § 21–4–102.

64. *See generally* Kurtis A. Kemper, *Determination that Child is Neglected or Dependent, or that Parental Rights Should be Terminated, on Basis that Parent Has Failed to Provide for Child's Education*, 6 A.L.R.6th 161 (2005) (discussing the cases that consider whether a child is neglected or whether parental rights should be terminated based on the failure of the parent to provide for the child's education).

65. *See generally* Jack Macmullan, Comment, *The Constitutionality of State Home Schooling Statutes*, 39 Vill. L. Rev. 1309 (1994) (discussing the various state approaches to home schooling).

66. *See* Ariz. Rev. Stat. Ann. § 15–802(B)(1); Ark. Code Ann. §§ 6–15–501 to -507; Colo. Rev. Stat. Ann. §§ 22–33–104, -104.5; D.C. Code Ann. § 31–402; Fla. Stat. Ann. § 1002.41; Ga. Code Ann. § 20–2–690.1; Iowa Code Ann. §§ 299.1, 299A.1; La. Rev. Stat. Ann. §§ 17:236, 236.1; Minn. Stat. Ann. § 120A.22(Subd. 4); Miss. Code Ann. s. 37–13–91; Mo. Ann. Stat. § 167.031; Mont. Stat. Ann. § 20–5–102; N.H. Rev. Stat. Ann. § 193:1(I)(b); N.M. Stat. Ann. § 22–12–2; N.C. Gen. Stat. § 115C-564; N.D. Cent. Code § 15.1–20–02; N.Y. Educ. Law §3204(2); Ohio Rev. Code Ann. § 3321.04(A)(2); Or. Rev. Stat. s. 339.030(1)(d); Pa. Stat. Ann. tit. 24, § 13–1327(d); R.I. Gen. Laws § 16–19–1; S.C. Code Ann. § 59–65–40; Tenn. Code Ann. § 49–6–3001(c)(2)(C); Vt. Stat. Ann. tit. 16, § 1121; Va. Code Ann. § 22.1–254; Wash. Rev. Code Ann. s. 28A.225.010; W. Va. Code § 18–8–1(c); Wis. Stat. Ann. § 118.15(4); Wyo. Stat. § 21–4–102(b).

67. *See* Macmullan, *supra* note 65, at 1342–49 (discussing the various requirements that states may have: notification and approval requirements, time and curriculum requirements, teacher qualifications, and assessment requirements).

68. Alaska Stat. § 14.30.010(b)(11); Conn. Gen. Stat. Ann. § 10–184; Del. Code Ann. tit. 14, § 2703; Idaho Code § 33–202; Ind. Code Ann. § 20–8.1–3–34; Ind. Code Ann. § 20–33–2–8; Me. Rev. Stat. Ann. tit. 20-A, § 5001-A(3); Md. code Ann., Educ. § 7–301(a); Mass. Gen. Laws Ann. ch. 76, § 1; Nev. Rev. Stat. Ann. § 392.070; N.J. Stat. Ann. § 18A :38–25; Okla. Stat. Ann. tit. 70, § 10–105; S.D. Codified Laws Ann. § 13–27–3.

69. Ala. Code §§ 16–28–1, -3; Cal. Educ. Code §§ 48222; Ill. Ann. Stat. ch. 105, para. 5/26–1(1); Kan. Stat. Ann. § 72–1111; Ky. Rev. Stat. Ann. § 159.030(1)(b); Mich. Comp. Laws Ann. § 380.1561(3)(a); Neb. Rev. Stat. § 79–201(b); Tex. Educ. Code Ann. § 21.086.

70. Neb. Rev. Stat. § 79–201(b) (stating "Every person residing in a school district within the state of Nebraska who has legal or actual charge of any child who is of mandatory attendance age ... shall cause such child to enroll in ... and attend regularly a public, private, denominational or parochial day school which meets the requirements for legal operation"); see also Macmullan, supra note 65, at 1340 (discussing the requirements in Alabama, Kansas, Michigan, and Nebraska for home schools).

71. Ala. Code §§ 16–28–1 (defining a private school as "only such schools as hold a certificate issued by the State Superintendent of Education" and stating that "instruction in such schools shall be by persons holding certificates issued by the State Superintendent of Education").

72. U.S. Department of Education National Center for Education Statistics, Issue Brief: 1.1 Million Homeschooled Students in the United States in 2003 (July 2004), available at http://nces.ed.gov/pubs2004/2004115.pdf (last visited on March 10, 2008).

73. See generally Michael Brian Dailey, Home Schooled Children Gaining Limited Access to Public Schools, 28 J.L. & Educ. 25 (1999) (discussing the various cases and statutes concerning home-school student access to extracurricular activities); see also Derwin L. Webb, Home-Schools and Interscholastic Sports: Denying Participation Violates United States Constitutional Due Process and Equal Protection, 26 J.L. & Educ. 123 (1997).

74. See e.g., McNatt v. Frazier Sch. Dist., 1995 WL 565380 (W.D. Pa. March 10, 1995) (holding that the denial of participation on a public school baseball team to a 14-year-old home-schooled child did not offend the Constitution); Bradstreet v. Sobal, 630 N.Y.S.2d 486 (N.Y. 1995) (holding that a regulation that provided that only students who regularly attended a public school could participate in interscholastic sports did not violate the Fourteenth Amendment).

75. See, e.g., Idaho Code § 33–203 (allowing a child to be enrolled in the public school system for "dual enrollment purposes," thus allowing the child to participate in public school activities if the student complies with all of the requirements of regularly enrolled children and achieves a minimum score on the state board of education annual achievement test).

76. NASW, People with Disabilities, supra note 1, at 288.

77. Id.

78. 20 U.S.C. § 1412(a)(1).

79. Id. at 1401(9).

80. Id. at § 1401(26). § 1401(26) states:

    The term 'related services' means transportation, and such developmental, corrective, and other supportive services (including speech pathology and audiology, psychological services, physical and occupational therapy, recreation, including therapeutic recreation, social work services, including rehabilitation counseling, and medical services, except that such medical services shall be for diagnostic and evaluation purposes only) as may be required to assist a child with a disability to benefit from special education, and includes the early identification and assessment of disabling conditions in children.

81. Id. at 1401(9)(D).

82. This means that even if the public school system places the child in a private school, they are still responsible for supervising that placement and ensuring its continued appropriateness.

83. Ann K. Wooster, What Constitutes Services That Must Be Provided by Federally Assisted Schools Under the Individuals with Disabilities Education Act, 161 A.L.R. Fed. 1, § 3 (2005) (citing Individuals with Disabilities Education Act, 20 U.S.C. § 601[d][1][A]; Todd v. Duneland Sch. Corp, 299 F.3d 899, 905 [7th Cir. 2002]).

84. Disputes over what constitutes required services have included: "an aide, behavior management, extra schooldays or year-round education, extracurricular activity, a full school day, physical education, services for a child voluntarily enrolled by parents at a private school, specialized teacher training, transition services, [and] transportation within or without the school district or state in connection with special education." Wooster, supra note 83 at § 2[a].

85. 20 U.S.C. 1412(a)(5).

86. 34 C.F.R. 300.114.

87. *Id. See also* Brian L. Porto, *Application of 20 U.S.C.A. § 1412(A), Least Restrictive Environment Provision of Individuals with Disabilities Education Act (IDEA), 20 U.S.C.A. §§ 1400 et seq.*, 189 A.L.R. Fed. 297, § 2 (2003–2004).

88. Rehabilitation Act, 29 U.S.C. § 794 (stating that "[n]o otherwise qualified individual with a disability in the United States ... shall, solely by reason of her or his disability, be excluded from the participation in, be denied the benefits of, or be subjected to discrimination under any program or activity receiving Federal financial assistance ...); Americans with Disabilities Act, 42 U.S.C. § 12132 (stating that "no qualified individual with a disability shall, by reason of such disability, be excluded from participation in or be denied the benefits of the services, programs, or activities of a public entity, or be subjected to discrimination by any such entity").

89. 34 C.F.R. § 104.44(a).

90. 28 C.F.R. § 35.130(b)(7).

91. *See generally* Richard E. Kaye, *What Constitutes Reasonable Accommodation Under Federal Statutes Protecting Rights of Disabled Individual, as Regards Educational Program or School Rules as Applied to Learning Disabled Student*, 166 A.L.R. Fed. 503 (2000–2005) (discussing the various cases where accommodations or modifications were or were not found reasonable).

92. *Id.* at § 2.

93. *See generally* Heidi Hoffecker Andry, Note, *Civil Rights Law—Right to a Free Appropriate Public Education Under the Individuals with Disabilities Education Act—Reimbursement for Private School Tuition*, 62 Tenn. L. Rev. 313 (1995) (discussing the various cases concerning reimbursement for private school tuition in these circumstances).

94. *Burlington Sch. Comm. V. Dept. of Educ.*, 471 U.S. 359 (1985).

95. Andry, *supra* note 93, at 324–25.

96. *Florence Cty. Sch. Dist. Four v. Carter*, 510 U.S. 7 (1993).

97. *Id.* at 14–16.

98. *See Bd. of Educ. of City Sch. Dist. of City of New York v. Tom F.*, 128 S.Ct 1 (2007).

99. Debra M. Hernandez Jozefowicz, Paula Allen-Meares, Mariann A. Piro-Lupinacci, & Randy Fisher, *School Social Work in the United States: A Holistic Approach, in* School Social Work Worldwide 33, 39 (Marion Huxtable & Eric Blythe eds., 2002).

100. *Id.*

101. Charlene Thiede, *Social Workers Assist in Reducing Disparities in Special Education*, 4 Intersections in Practice 3, 3 (2005), *available at* http://www.socialworkers.org (last visited on April 1, 2008).

102. *Id.*

103. *Id.* at 5.

104. *See* Jozefowicz, et al., *supra* note 99, at 39.

105. Elizabeth M. Timberlake & Christine Anlauf Sabatino, *Individuals with Disabilities Education Act: Translating and Implementing, in* The School Services Guidebook: A Guide for School-Based Professionals, *supra* note 13, at 897–898.

106. *Id.* at 901.

107. *Id.* at 894.

108. Office of English Language Acquisition, National Clearinghouse for English Language Acquisition & Language Instruction Educational Programs, *NCELA Frequently Asked Questions, available at* http://www.ncela.gwu.edu/expert/faq/ (last visited on March 3, 2008) [hereinafter NCELA FAQ].

109. *Id.*

110. NASW, *Linguistic/Cultural Diversity in the United States, supra* note 1, at 250.

111. *Lau v. Nichols*, 414 U.S. 563 (1974).

112. *Id.* at 568.

113. *See* NASW, *Linguistic/Cultural Diversity in the United States, supra* note 1, at 250.

114. *Id.* at 238.

115. *See* NCELA FAQ, *supra* note 108.

116. *Id.*

117. *See, e.g.,* NASW, *Linguistic/Cultural Diversity in the United States, supra* note 1, at 251.

118. *See* NCELA FAQ, *supra* note 108.

119. *Plyler v. Doe* at 223.

120. *Id.*

121. 20 U.S.C. § 6301 (2002).

122. Nina Rabin, Mary Carol Combs, & Norma Gonzalez, *Understanding Plyler's Legacy: Voices from Border Schools,* 37 J. L. & Educ. 15, 53 (2008).

123. *Id.* at 54–56.

124. NASW, *Immigrants and Refugees, supra* note 1, at 227.

125. Joy Wawrzyniak & Amie Anger, *Faces and Voices of Refugee Youths,* School Social Work: Section Connection 8, 8 (Spring 2004).

126. Gilberto Perez, *Helping Latino Immigrant Students Adjust: The Bienvenido Acculturation Program,* School Social Work: Section Connection 1, 10–11 (Summer 2005).

127. NASW, *Lesbian, Gay, and Bisexual Issues, supra* note 1, at 247.

128. NASW, *Transgender and Gender Identity Issues, supra* note 1, at 368.

129. NASW, *Education of Children and Youths, supra* note 1, at 115.

130. NASW, *School Violence, supra* note 1, at 337.

131. *Id.*

132. *Id.*

133. 514 F.3d 87, 91 (1st Cir. 2008).

134. NASW, *Education of Children and Youths, supra* note 1, at 117.

135. *Parker,* 514 F.3d at 90.

136. *Id.*

137. *Id.* at 94.

138. *Id.* at 106.

139. ACLU Sues Florida High School for Suppressing Free Speech, January 31, 2008, http://www.aclu.org/lgbt/youth/33864prs20080131.html (Gillman v. Holmes County School District, case no. 5:08-cv-34, U.S. District Court of the Northern District of Florida, Panama City Division. This case is currently unreported.)

140. Federal Judge Rules that Students Can't be Barred From Expressing Their Support for Gay People, May 13, 2008, http://www.aclu.org/lgbt/youth/35265prs20080513.html

141. *Id.*

142. *Id.*

143. *Id.* This decision is currently unreported. ACLU, *supra* note 139.

144. Tinker v. Des Moines Indep. Cmty. Sch. Dist, 393 U.S. 503, 506 (1969).

145. *See* Brief for Amicus, NASW at 13–14, *East High Gay/Straight Alliance v. Board of Educ. of Salt Lake City School Dist.,* 30 F.Supp.2d 1356 (D.Utah 1998).

146. *Id.* at 15.

147. 20 U.S.C. 4071

148. Board of Education of the Westside Community Schools v. Mergens, 496 U.S. 226, 239 (1990).

149. *Id.* at 240.

150. *Id.*

151. *Id.*

152. 258 F.Supp.2d 667, 675 (E.D.Ky. 2003).

153. *Id.*

154. *Id.* at 676.

155. *Id.* at 677.

156. *Id.* at 687–88.

157. *Boyd County High School GSA,* 258 F.Supp.2d at 678.

158. *Id* at 687–88.

159. For a discussion on how schools may try to avoid triggering EAA protections see Brian Berkley, *Making Gay Straight Alliance Student Groups Curriculum-Related: A New Tactic for Schools Trying to Avoid the Equal Access Act,* 61 Wash. & Lee L. Rev. 1847 (2004).

160. 83 F.Supp.2d 1135 (C.D.Cal. 2000)

161. *Id.* at 1143.

162. *Id.*

163. *Id.* at 1144.

164. *Id.*

165. *Colin,* 83 F.Supp.2d at 1144.

166. *Id.* at 1149.

167. Board of Regents of the University of Wisconsin, et al., v. Scott Harold Southworth, 529 U.S. 217 (2000).

168. *Id.* at 221.

169. *See* Brief for Amicus, NASW, *Nabozny v. Podlesny,* et al., 92 F.3d 446, 451–53 (7th Cir. 1996) (citing Paul Gibson, Gay Male and Lesbian Youth Suicide, in Report of the Secretary's Task Force on Youth Suicide, 3–110 (U.S. Dept. of Health & Human Services Pub. No. (ADM) 89–1623, 1989).

170. 92 F.3d 446, 451–53 (7th Cir. 1996).

171. *Id.* at 451.

172. *Id.*

173. *See* Brief for Amicus, NASW, *Nabozny v. Podlesny,* et al., 92 F.3d 446, 451–53 (7th Cir. 1996).

174. *Nabozny,* 92 F.3d at 460.

175. NASW, *Education of Children and Youths, supra* note 1, at 117.

176. NASW, *Cultural and Linguistic Competence in the Social Work Profession, supra* note 1, at 80.

177. *See id.* at 81.

178. *Id.*

179. 539 U.S. 244 (2003).

180. 539 U.S. 306 (2003).

181. *Gratz,* 539 U.S. at 255

182. *Id.* at 256

183. *Id.* at 251–52.

184. *Id.* at 270.

185. *Id.*

186. *Id.* at 275–76.

187. *Gratz,* 539 U.S. at 271–72.

188. *Id.* at 271–75.

189. *Grutter,* 539 U.S. at 315–16.

190. *Id.*

191. *Id.* at 335–36.

192. *Id.* at 337.

193. *Id.* at 343.

194. *Parents Involved in Comm. Schools v. Seattle School Dist. No. 1* and *Meredith v. Jefferson County Board of Educ.,* 127 S.Ct. 2738 (2007).

195. *Id.* at 2740–41.

196. It should be noted that the Supreme Court's decision that there is no compelling interest in pursuing diversity in public schools on the basis of race does not disturb the Court's holding in *Grutter v. Bollinger,* 539 U.S. 306 (2003). *Id.* at 2753–54. *Parents Involved in Comm. Schools,* 127 S.Ct. at 2753–54.

197. *See* Sherri Morgan and Carolyn I. Polowy, *A Review of the Supreme Court's 2007 Affirmative Action Decision,* NASW Legal Defense Fund Legal Issue of the Month, September 2007 at 2. (indicating that the opinion of Justice Kennedy is considered by many scholars to have the legal gravity of a majority opinion since it was Kennedy's swing vote that achieved the votes necessary to hand down a decision).

198. *Parents Involved in Comm. Schools,* 127 S.Ct. at 2790.

199. *Id.* at 2792.

200. NASW, *Gender, Ethnic, and Race-Based Workplace Discrimination, supra* note 1, at 176.

201. NASW, *Education of Children and Youths, supra* note 1, at 117.

202. 20 U.S.C. 1681(a) (1988).

203. A "recipient" of federal funding is "any State or political subdivision thereof, or any instrumentality of a State or political subdivision thereof, any public or private agency, institution, or organization, or other entity, or any person, to whom Federal financial assistance is extended directly or through another recipient and which operates an education program or activity which receives such assistance, including any subunit, successor, assignee, or transferee thereof" 34 C.F.R. 106.2(i) (current through June 26, 2008).

204. 43 F.3d 265, 268 (6th Cir. 1994).

205. *Id.*

206. *Id.* at 270.

207. *Id.* at 271.

208. *Id.*

209. *Id.* at 271–72.

210. 134 F.Supp.2d 965, 967 (N.D. Ill. 2001).

211. *Id.*

212. *Id.*

213. *Id.* at 970.

214. *Brenden v. Independent School Dist.,* 477 F.2d 1292, 1298 (8th Cir. 1973).

215. 34 C.F.R. § 106.41(c) (current through June 26, 2008). There are several factors that must be considered in order to determine if equal athletic opportunities are actually available: "(1) Whether the selection of sports and levels of competition effectively accommodate the interests and abilities of members of both sexes; (2) The provision of equipment and supplies; (3) Scheduling of games and practice time; (4) Travel and per diem allowance; (5) Opportunity to receive coaching and academic tutoring; (6) Assignment and compensation of coaches and tutors; (7) Provision of locker rooms, practice and competitive facilities; (8) Provision of medical and training facilities and services; (9) Provision of housing and dining facilities and services; (10) Publicity." *Id.*

216. Gonyo v. Drake University, 837 F.Supp. 989, 994 (S.D. Iowa 1993).

217. 370 F.3d 275, 280 (2nd Cir. 2004).

218. *Id.*

219. *Id.*

220. *Id.* at 302

221. *See* 176 F.R.D. 220 (W.D. Va. 1997).

222. 985 F.Supp. 1458 (M.D. Fla. 1997).

223. 858 F.2d 579 (9th Cir. 1988).

224. *Daniels v. School Bd. of Brevard County, Fla.*, 995 F.Supp. 1394 (M.D. Fla 1997).

225. National Center for Education Statistics, Bureau of Justice Statistics, *Indicators of School Crime and Safety: 2003, available at* http://nces.ed.gov/pubs2004/2004004.pdf (last visited on March 10, 2008) (stating that "violence, theft, bullying, drugs, and firearms are still prevalent: students ages 12–18 were victims of 764,000 violent crimes and 1.2 million crimes of theft at school in 2001"). For a list of school violence research findings see North Carolina Department of Juvenile Justice and Delinquency Prevention—Center for the Prevention of School Violence, *Stats 2003: Selected School Violence Research Findings from 2003 Sources, available at* http://www.ncdjjdp.org/cpsv/pdf_files/Stats_2003.pdf (last visited on March 3, 2008).

226. NASW, *School Violence, supra* note 1, at 316.

227. *Id.* at 316–317; *see also*, National Association of Social Workers, *NASW Standards for School Social Work Services* 16 (2002), *available at* http://www.naswdc.org (last visited on April 28, 2008).

228. NASW, *School Violence, supra* note 1, at 316.

229. *Id.*

230. *See generally* Allan E. Korpela, *Tort Liability of Public Schools and Institutions of Higher Learning for Injuries Caused by Acts of Fellow Students*, 36 A.L.R.3d 330 (1971–2005) (discussing the various cases where courts have and have not found liability based on location of the incident).

231. 20 U.S.C. §§ 1681(a) (1988). Title IX reads: "No person in the United States shall, on the basis of sex, be excluded from participation in, be denied the benefits of, or be subjected to discrimination under any education program or activity receiving Federal financial assistance." *Id.*

232. 42 U.S.C. § 1983.

233. *See* Robin Cheryl Miller, *Liability, Under State Law Claims, of Public and Private Schools and Institutions of Higher Learning for Teacher's, Other Employee's, or Student's Sexual Relationship with, or Sexual Harassment or Abuse of, Student*, 86 A.L.R.5th 1, §§ 15, 18 (2001–2005) (discussing the state tort liability of public and private schools for the harassment or abuse of a student by another student).

234. *See supra* note 231.

235. *See* Sandra Kopels & David R. Dupper, *School-Based Peer Sexual Harassment*, 78 CHILD WELFARE 435,441–42 (1999).

236. *See* Kristen M. Eriksson, *What Our Children Are Really Learning in School: Using Title IX to Combat Peer Sexual Harassment*, 83 Geo. L.J. 1799 (1995) (arguing that Title IX should be used to hold school districts liable for peer on peer sexual harassment); Jeff Horner, *A Student's Right to Protection from Violence and Sexual Abuse in the School Environment*, 36 S. Tex. L. Rev. 45 (1995) (discussing the early claims brought by students under Title IX).

237. *Franklin v. Gwinnett County Public Schools*, 503 U.S. 60, 65, and 74–75 (1992).

238. *Id.* at 76.

239. *See infra* "Confidentiality Dilemmas" pp. 50.

240. For a discussion of various cases concerning the matter, see Belinda Bean, *Right of Action Under Title IX of Education Amendments Act of 1972 (20 U.S.C.A. §§ 1681 et seq.) Against School or School District for Sexual Harassment of Student by Student's Peers*, 141 A.L.R. Fed. 407, § 3[a](1997–2005).

241. *Davis v. Monroe Cty. Bd. of Educ.*, 526 U.S. 629 (1999).

242. *Id.* at 638–53. *See also Murrell v. Sch. Dist. No. 1*, 186 F.3d 1238 (10th Cir. 1999). NASW joined an amicus brief in support of the high school student in this case, stating that the proper standard in a peer sexual harassment claim under Title IX is whether the school has "ratified the discriminatory harassment based on sex when they knew or should have known of a hostile environment and yet failed to take appropriate corrective action." *Murrell*, Amicus Curiae Brief of the National Association of School Psychologists, et al., In Support of Plaintiff-Appellant (No. 97–1055) at 1 [hereinafter *Murrell* Amicus Brief].

243. Kopels & Dupper, *supra* note 235, at 451–52.

244. Horner, *supra* note 236, at 46–7.

245. *Walton v. Alexander*, 20 F.3d 1350 (5th Cir. 1994).

246. Horner, *supra* note 236, at 54.

247. *Murrell* at 1238.

248. *Id.* at 1252. *See Murrell* Amicus Brief for a discussion of NASW's position in support of the high school student in this case.

249. *Murrell* Amicus Brief at 53.

250. Miller, *supra* note 233, at § 15[a] (discussing the cases where tort liability of the school district was found for the harassment of a student by another student on the ground that the school authorities negligently supervised the students).

251. *Id.* at § 18; *see, e.g., Nicole M. v. Martinez Unified Sch. Dist.*, 964 F. Supp. 1369 (N.D. Cal. 1997).

252. Kopels & Dupper, *supra* note 235, at 454.

253. *Id.*

254. *Id.* See Kopels and Dupper at 454–58 for a detailed discussion of intervention steps that social workers can use to actually prevent peer sexual harassment.

255. NASW, *School Violence, supra* note 1, at 333.

256. *Id.* at 336.

257. Office of the Surgeon General, *Youth Violence: A Report of the Surgeon General* (2001), *available at* http://www.surgeongeneral.gov/library/youthviolence (last visited on March 3, 2008).

258. NASW, *School Violence, supra* note 1, at 339; *see also* National Association of Social Workers, *Youth Bullying ... How Social Workers Can Help* (2003).

259. NASW, *School Violence, supra* note 1, at 334–5.

260. *See* Alexander C. Black, *Search Conducted by School Official or Teacher as Violation of Fourth Amendment or Equivalent State Constitutional Provision*, 31 A.L.R.5th 229 (1995–2005).

261. U.S. Const. Amend. IV ("The right of the people to be secure in their persons, houses, papers, and effects, against unreasonable searches and seizures, shall not be violated, and no Warrant shall issue, but upon probable cause, supported by Oath or affirmation, and particularly describing the place to be searched, and the persons to be seized").

262. *Tinker v. Des Moines Independent Community Sch. Dist.*, 393 U.S. 503, 506 (1969).

263. *New Jersey v. T.L.O.*, 469 U.S. 325, 333 (1985). The Fourth Amendment, however, does not extend to private school officials. *Vernonia v. Acton*, 515 U.S. 646, 653 (1995).

264. *Smyth v. Lubbers*, 398 F.Supp 777, 785 (W.D.Mich 1975). This decision regarding majority-age college students, however, has not been yet applied to elementary or secondary schoolchildren.

265. *State v. Engerud*, 463 A.2d 934, 943 (N.J. 1983) But this has not been addressed by the U.S. Supreme Court.

266. *T.L.O.* at 337–338.

267. *Id.* at 341–342.

268. *Id.* at 341–342 (citing *Terry v. Ohio*, 392 U.S. 1, 20 (1968)).

269. *Id.* at 342. Individualized suspicion made a search reasonable, however it may not be required. In some cases, for example drug testing of sports teams, individualized suspicion is not required. *See Bd. of Educ. of Indep. Sch. Dist. No. 92 of Pottawatomie Cty. v. Earls*, 536 U.S. 822, 830 (2002); *Vernonia v. Acton* at 653.

270. However, consent may not be sufficient in the case of students whose consent may not be fully voluntary because of fear. *Tarter v. Raybuck*, 742 F.2d 977, 980–981 (6th Cir. 1984).

271. *T.L.O.* at 341.

272. *Redding v. Safford Unified Sch. Dist, #1, et al.*, 531 F.3d 1071, 2008 WL 2648101 (9th Cir. 2008).

273. *Redding v. Safford Unified Sch. Dist. #1, et al.*, 504 F.3d 828, 830–831 (9th Cir. 2007).

274. *Id.* at 831.

275. *Redding*, 531 F.3d 1071 at *1080-1085.

276. *Id.* at 1085-1089.

277. *Safford Unified Sch. Dist. #1 v. Redding*, 129 S. Ct. 2633 *2642 (2009).

278. Kathleen M. Dorr, *Validity, Under Federal Constitution, of Regulations, Rules, or Statutes Allowing Drug Testing of Students*, 87 A.L.R. Fed. 148, § 2 (1988–2004).

279. *See, e.g.*, *Bd. of Educ. of Indep. Sch. Dist. No. 92 of Pottawatomie Cty. v. Earls*.

280. *Earls* at 838 (stating that the policy "was a reasonable means of furthering the School District's important interest in preventing and deterring drug use among its schoolchildren" and therefore did not violate the Fourth Amendment). NASW joined an amicus brief in support of the high school students in this case. It was NASW's position that the policy of requiring all students who participated in competitive extracurricular activities to submit to drug testing violates the Fourth Amendment and is contrary to demonstrated evidence that there is a "strong association between student extracurricular involvement and abstinence from drugs." *Earls*, Brief of Amici Curiae American Academy of Pediatrics, et al., In Support of Respondents at *4 (No. 01–332), *available at* 2002 WL 206367 [hereinafter *Earls Amicus Brief*].

281. *Tannahill ex rel. Lockney Indep. Sch.Dist.*, 515 U.S. 646 (1995).

282. Dorr, *supra* note 278, at § 3.

283. NASW, *School Truancy and Dropout Prevention*, *supra* note 1, at 328.

284. *E.g.*, U.S. companies lose an estimated $40 billion per year because of illiteracy. *Id.* at 327.

285. *Id.* at 330. Risk factors include: limited English proficiency, poverty, race, geographic location, or economic disadvantage. *Id.* at 328. Economic influences include: employed students, single parent homes, high mobility rates, parents with multiple jobs, and lack of affordable transportation and childcare. *Id.* at 327–8. Student variables include: drug and alcohol abuse, lack of understanding about attendance laws, lack of social competence, mental health difficulties, and poor physical health. *Id.* at 328.

286. *Id.* at 329.

287. John Wong, Amy Salomon, Lynda Thistle Elliott, Louis Tallarita, & Shelley Reed, Symposium, *The McKinney-Vento Homeless Assistance Act—Education for Homeless Children and Youths Program: Turning Good Law into Effective Education*, 11 Geo. J. on Poverty L. & Pol'y 283, 284 (2004).

288. *Id.*

289. *Id.*

290. JoAnn Grozuczak Goedert, Comment, *The Education of Homeless Children: The McKinney Act and its Implications*, 140 Ed. Law Rep. 9, 10 (2000).

291. *Id.*

292. *Id.*

293. 42 U.S.C. §§ 11431–11435 (2002).

294. *Id.* at § 11431.

295. *Id.*

296. Wong, et al., *supra* note 287.

297. Sheila O'Leary, *Educating Homeless Children*, 8 Geo. J. on Poverty L. & Pol'y 513, 515 (2001).

298. Andrea B. Berkowitz, Note, *Homeless Children Dream of College Too: The Struggle to Provide America's Homeless Youth with a Viable Education*, 31 Hofstra L. Rev. 515, 517 (2002).

299. *Id.* at 530–531.

300. *Id.*

301. *Id.* at 528–9.

302. *Id.*

303. Janis K. Doleschal, *Managing Risk in Interscholastic Athletic Programs: 14 Legal Duties of Care*, 17 Marq. Sports L. Rev. 295, 325 (2006).

304. National Highway Traffic Safety Administration, *Key Provisions of Occupant Restraint Laws through July 1, 2006, available at* http://www.nhtsa.dot.gov/people/injury/occupant_restraints_chart-4-3-06.pdf (last visited on March 11, 2008).

305. Doleschal, *supra* note 303, at 298.

306. David M. Vukadinovich, *Minors' Rights to Consent to Treatment: Navigating the Complexity of State Laws*, 37 J. Health L. 667 (2004).

307. *Id.* at 677–8.

308. *Id.*

309. *Id.*

310. Twenty states and the District of Columbia allow minors to consent to some outpatient mental health treatment. The Alan Guttmacher Institute, *Minors and the Right to Consent to Healthcare*, 2 Issues in Brief 1, 4 (2000).

311. Vukadinovich, *supra* note 306, at 682–3.

312. *Id.* at 668.

313. Guttmacher, *supra* note 310, at 5.

314. Barbara A. Weiner & Robert M. Wettstein, *Legal Issues in Mental Health Care* 218 (Plenum Press, 1993).

315. *Griswold v. Connecticut*, 381 U.S. 479 (1965); *Roe v. Wade*, 410 U.S. 959 (1973).

316. Weiner & Wettstein, *supra* note 314, at 218.

317. National Association of Social Workers, *Code of Ethics* § 1.07 (revised 1999) ("Privacy and Confidentiality"), *available at* http://www.socialworkers.org/pubs/code/code.asp (last visited on March 3, 2008).

318. *Id.*

319. *Id.*

320. *Education*, Statistical Abstract of the United States: 2004–2005, U.S. Census Bureau, *available at* http://www.census.gov/prod/2004pubs/04statab/educ.pdf (last visited on March 3, 2008).

321. Robert L. Barker, The Social Work Dictionary 335–36 (3rd ed. 1995) (emphasis removed).

322. Sandra Kopels & Brenda Coble Lindsey, *The Complexity of Confidentiality in Schools Today: The School Social Worker Context*, School Social Work Journal 463 (Summer 2006).

323. *Id.*

324. *Id.*

325. *See*, National Association of Social Workers Legal Defense Fund, *Social Workers & the Legal Rights of Children* (Part I: Family Matters) 5 (2007).

326. *Id.*

327. Weiner & Wettstein, *supra* note 314, at 219.

328. 20 U.S.C. § 1232g (2002).

329. Weiner & Wettstein, *supra* note 314, at 219.

330. *Id.*

331. *Id.*

332. National Association of Social Workers, *Code of Ethics* § 1.07(c) (revised 1999) ("Privacy and Confidentiality"), *available at* http://www.socialworkers.org/pubs/code/code.usp (last visited March 3, 2008).

333. *Id.*

334. *Id.*

335. Nic Dibble, *Wisconsin's School-Based Youth Suicide Prevention Initiative*, School Social Work: Section Connection 1, 1 (Spring 2005).

336. Laurie Emmer, *Youth Suicide: Prevention and Intervention for School Social Workers*, School Social Work: Practice Update 1, 2–3 (Winter 2005).

337. NASW, *Youth Suicide*, *supra* note 1, at 397.

338. *Tarasoff v. Regents of University of California*, 551 P.2d 334 (Cal. 1976).

339. Ann Hubbard, *Symposium: The Future of "The Duty to Protect": Scientific and Legal Perspectives on Tarasoff's 30th Anniversary*, 75 U. Cin. L. Rev. 429, 433 (2006).

340. 20 U.S.C. § 1232g (1974).

341. Dept. of Educ., *Balancing Student Privacy and School Safety: A Guide to the Family Educational Rights and Privacy Act for Elementary and Secondary Schools* (2007), *available at* http://www.ed.gov/print/policy/gen/guid/fpco/brochures/elsec/html (last visited on March 11, 2008).

342. *Id.*

343. *Id.*

344. *Id.*

345. *Id.*

346. Mary H.B. Gelfman, Commentary, *School Health Services and Educational Records: Conflicts in the Law*, 64 Ed. Law Rep. 319 (1991).

347. Kopels & Lindsey, *supra* note 322.

348. *See* N.C. ex rel. M.C. v. Bedford Central School Dist., 348 F.Supp.2d 32, 37 (2004).

349. *Id.*

350. Albers v. Breen, 806 N.E.2d 667, 672 (Ill. Ct. App. 2004).

351. *Id.*

352. Albers, 806 N.E.2d 667.

353. *Id.* at 672–73.

354. *Id.* at 673.

355. *See Id.*

356. *Port Washington Teachers' Ass'n v. Bd. of Educ. of the Port Washington Union Free Sch. Dist.*, 478 F.3d 494 (2d Cir. 2007).

357. *Id.*

358. *Port Washington*, Amicus Curiae Brief of the American Civil Liberties Union, et al., In Support of Plaintiff-Appellant (No. 06–0708-cv).

359. Melissa Prober, *Please Don't Tell My Parents*, 71 Brook. L. Rev. 557, 570 (2005).

360. *Id.* at 563.

361. *Id.* at 577.